All Christians Are Monks

The Monastery, the Parish and
the Renewal of the Church

— GEORGE GUIVER —

Sacristy Press
PO Box 612, Durham, DH1 9HT

www.sacristy.co.uk

First published in 2024 by Sacristy Press, Durham

Sacristy Limited, registered in England & Wales, number 7565667

British Library Cataloguing-in-Publication Data
A catalogue record for the book is available from the British Library

ISBN 978-1-78959-346-4

Contents

Acknowledgements...iv

Chapter 1. Monasteries and parishes—a shared world 1
Chapter 2. A day in the life of................................... 5
Chapter 3. Things, people, practices 19
Chapter 4. Community and communion 32
Chapter 5. It's genetic.. 56
Chapter 6. Practices 73
Chapter 7. More practices....................................... 90
Chapter 8. Going for effect.................................... 103
Chapter 9. Coming into focus 129
Chapter 10. Monastery and parish 144

For further reading... 152
Appendix: "Can these stones come alive?".................... 153

Acknowledgements

I am really grateful to those who read the text in part or whole and made their comments. My special thanks go to Carla Calvetti, Simon Crook, Stephen Platten, and my brethren Nicolas, John, Patrick, Charlie and Jude, all of whose comments were invaluable. Special thanks too to my brethren in the Abbey of St Matthias, Trier, for space to write; for access to the German Liturgical Institute, and the invaluable help of Andrea Bauer, its librarian; and to Ralf Schmitz for our fruitful conversations.

1

Monasteries and parishes—a shared world

The book's title should have been "all Christians are *nuns and monks*" of course, but titles need to be snappy, and one gender can't monopolize a word that traditionally applies to all people in that way of life. What I want to show is that the women and men who live and work in religious communities have something life-giving to share with contemporary Christians; furthermore, we may get a whiff in them of a clarion call to return to things we have lost or grown weak in. They are not saying in this, "We are better than you," but rather something like: "We've been given this amazing fruitcake—try a piece, and then if you want some more, go to the One who made it." The churches in the developed world are facing great challenges: many are working hard in quest of renewal but in an uphill struggle. My hope is that in reading this book you may begin to wonder if religious communities are on to something that can help find the way. This book is for Christians of all sorts: for folk in parishes and local church communities and for religious communities themselves. The title is partly ironic, but it is not saying anything new: there is a strand in the Orthodox churches of the East, for instance, which says all Christians participate in the life of monks and nuns. If you read on, you may find the idea to be not so strange as it sounds.

Stepping into a world

I find myself going back to my childhood. My brother John and I sang in the choir of St Paul's Leicester. We went to church three times every Sunday, and four times once we were confirmed: 8 o'clock Mass with Communion, 11 o'clock non-communicating High Mass, 3 o'clock

Young People's Church, and 6.30 Solemn Evensong, and we took the eight twenty-minute walks between home and church for granted. The beautiful worship at St Paul's exercised my imagination, but I became conscious at the same time that it was marginal. The secular world seemed indifferent. This may have been coloured by my own insecurities at the time, but it has left me all my life with a strong awareness of a dichotomy: on the one hand the life-giving community and teaching and practice experienced in church, and on the other the persuasive "common sense" of the secular world, apparently achieved without reference to the Church and its life. After school I worked in a shop for a year before going to university, and was given a week's holiday in February. I had the daft idea to cycle from Leicester to Berwick-on-Tweed and back while it snowed.

Having been fascinated by a TV programme about it, on the return journey I arranged to stay at the Anglican Franciscan friary at Alnmouth in Northumberland. I had never been anywhere like this before: the brothers, committed to each other and to God, the chapel with its powerful atmosphere, a sense of divine mystery in the services, the beautiful setting looking out to sea, the simplicity, polished floors, simple food, and apparent lack of any heating. It was as if my normal experience of church, itself strong and life-giving, had been distilled into something more powerful. This is one effect that religious communities can have on us, touching the imagination and affections, and shifting our perceptions of things. Over the years that followed I was repeatedly to find myself drifting towards the "common sense" of a secular world that seems able to achieve so much more than the Church, only to be pulled back with a jolt each time I stayed in a monastery or convent. Here are two themes of this book: the powerful norm-setting of contemporary society, and the powerful experience of encounter in visiting a monastery.

More to it than you may think

Monastic life is unfamiliar to most people, and it will help first of all to say something about it. The word "monastic" is used broadly in this book—some communities are more monastic than others, and while people easily imagine monasteries and convents, we need to include many communities of sisters and brothers who don't live in such places, but have more informal modes of community life, very often geared to ways of service in society, with the poor, in education, medicine, and other ways. The life of the community founded by St Teresa of Calcutta, for instance, and its heroic work among the poor, is very different from the seclusion and prayer found in a Cistercian monastery. The variety is endless, from Eastern Orthodox monasteries we might visit in Greece or Russia to a modern Lutheran community that runs a pop group,[1] from small groups of sisters living in a house hidden away in a poor neighbourhood to courageous nuns rescuing trafficked girls from the Mafia in southern Italy. There are central things in the life of all of them which mean they are living the same life. A peculiarity of the English language is that "monastery" is thought to be male, and "convent" female—this is a misuse of the terms, and in all other languages they are interchangeable. So I always use the words "monastery" and "convent" in a unisex way, as they are in all other languages. I use the word "monastic" similarly as a shorthand umbrella term for all this great variety of monastic, active and missionary communities of brothers and sisters and people of every kind.

I am also using the term "parish" as an umbrella term to cover all Christian worshipping communities: churches, chaplaincies, and other groupings, all local groups of Christians committed to worshipping together—they are all "parishes", which means households of God. It comes from a Greek word for a household of people sharing the same life—and that sounds in fact just like a monastery. Parish and monastery are two of a kind, a theme that comes up repeatedly as we proceed.

The monastic world

Few people are aware of the dimensions of the monastic world. When you step into it, you step to your surprise into a landscape that is big. To illustrate this, we could take that beautiful, gentle animal the elephant, whose numbers have been shrinking at an alarming rate

---

[1] The Christusträger Bruderschaft

in recent decades. Religious brothers and sisters wouldn't at all mind being compared with such a gentle and peaceful animal. It is seen as a matter of concern that there are now fewer than 500,000 elephants in the world. If an elephant averages 5 m in length and 2.5 m in width, then standing shoulder-to-shoulder all those elephants would cover about 6,250,000 square metres, which is 1,545 acres. London's Hyde Park, whose area is huge, covers 350 acres—only a small part of the world's remaining elephants could get in it shoulder-to-shoulder. We can hardly envisage what a crowd of 500,000 elephants would look like. And yet their numbers are thought to be dangerously small. Similarly, religious brothers and sisters have decreased dramatically since the mid-twentieth century, and they might also be thought to be on the way out: it is a bit early to assume that. Counted altogether, Roman Catholic, Eastern Orthodox, Anglican, Lutheran, and Reformed brothers and sisters still tot up to over 1 million—twice the number of elephants; we don't have to work out how many monastics would fit into Hyde Park to envisage quite a multitude. In the Church, they are a great iceberg—they get on quietly without publicizing themselves, and hardly peep above the surface. However, our interest is not in numbers, strength, power or influence, which don't count for anything in monastic life, but in the sheer spread and variety of this world of thought and experience. The aim is not to impress with size, but to demonstrate that any assumption that this is a small sideshow needs some correction. The volume of monastic publications internationally can hardly be kept up with, the number of journals and books will surprise anyone who enquires, and they will be similarly amazed at the wealth of experience to be found in communities: knowledge of life on the street, amongst the disadvantaged, in education, pastoral work and other fields. It is a big and experienced world, full of amazing riches, but it never proclaims itself, and its nature is quietly to get on with the everyday without fanfare.

In order to get a handle on this, it will help to respond first of all to the frequent question, "What do you do all day?" In the next chapter, I attempt a sketch of life in my own community at Mirfield. No two communities are the same; timings and practices will vary, but what follows will begin to give some idea of how life shapes out in a community in the Benedictine tradition.

2

A day in the life of . . .

The alarm clock rings in time to get to Mattins at 6.45 a.m. Negotiating a long series of corridors and staircases that seem so brightly lit for newly-opened eyes, or, weather permitting, drinking deep fresh air through the outside route, I and my brothers get ourselves to our seats in choir to the sound of ringing bells and the gradual turning-on of church lights.

Morning

At 6.45 the Angelus bell rings (three threes and a nine). All stand, while any stragglers freeze on the spot wherever they are, waiting until the opening refrains of Mattins are done before they can come into choir to take their place. This journeying to church has been accomplished in the Greater Silence which lasts through the night until 9 a.m. In it no one speaks, unless it is unavoidably necessary to exchange a few quiet words about something. God is in the silence, God and us; you could say the silence is a music.

The choir (that is, the formal seating where we take our places) is the engine room of the ship, consisting at Mirfield of two rows of seats facing each other. Four times a day we are here, seven days a week, singing hymns and Psalms, the bread and butter of Daily Prayer in the Christian tradition in both monasteries and parishes. After some opening verses and refrains we sing a hymn and then sit down to sing a few Psalms. There is no instrumental accompaniment, and work is needed in order to sing together—over the years this builds up an intuitive togetherness, and a familiarity with the chant. Almost the entire community are non-musicians, making this easy familiarity with a large repertoire unusual.

It is never perfect, and occasionally a bit rough; the words and music are not anything you would want to sit down and listen to on Classic FM, and you can't explain why it is so fruitful to be doing it. A lot goes on in each brother during this singing: reflecting on the texts; thinking of things and people suggested by the text; the sufferings and challenges faced constantly by people the world over, whose voices are there all through the Psalms; the mind wandering sometimes; consciousness of our interdependence as a family; the things that cheer or exasperate me about my brothers; and above all our quest for God and God's low-key presence and voice coming to meet us. The Psalms follow a four-week cycle—once we get to the end of the cycle, back we go again to the beginning, revisiting again and again the same texts, the same music, the same hinterland. There are variations for special days and festivals, a dab of jam on the daily bread. In winter, we start surrounded by dark, the black windows gradually turning to blue with dawn's slow and grudging arrival. The contrasting perpetual light of summer is exhilarating—in our timetable you rarely see darkness in summer unless you stay up late. All the year through there is meanwhile a base rock of tacit knowledge—we are not alone, but are acting with millions all over the world in the same journey, as well as the company of the redeemed in heaven.

At the end of each Psalm, we bow in our seats for "Glory to the Father, and to the Son, and to the Holy Spirit . . . " and, as the singing finally comes to its end, books are put down while a brother gets up to read a passage from the Bible. This is followed by two minutes of silence. One might cough, another drop something, but mainly you could hear a pin drop. We stand to sing the Canticle, which is the same every day of the year, and after that a brother leads us in the prayers of the day, praying for a range of things that are the same every week. The service ends with us all saying the Lord's Prayer, the presider reading the Collect—the prayer for the day—and a blessing. We all turn towards the altar, bow and file out.

Breakfast and prayer

You could think of the medieval clock in Wells Cathedral where, on every hour, clockwork manikins go through the same performance, endlessly and identically repeated. If so, we will leave you with that impression for now, for the main purpose of this chapter is simply to describe, so far as we can, what happens. After that we will dig below the surface. As the procession of brothers winds out of sight, it carries on into the sacristy, where we form a circle. We go round the circle hearing of whatever is to happen this day, dealing with necessary arrangements and announcements. All disperse, still in silence. At some point, two things now happen: making for the refectory to eat some breakfast, and spending some time, at least 30 minutes, in private prayer. These can be in either order, according to choice. Breakfast is usually silent, and a peculiarly Anglican practice is the possibility of reading a book at silent meals; visitors using our library can sometimes happen upon marmalade deposits on theological books, or dabs of porridge, something that can infuriate the librarian. For myself, it is usually a time for reading either *The Week* or *The Economist* to catch up with what the world is doing.

The time of silent prayer can be where you choose, in church, in your room, or elsewhere. It can take all manner of forms, but it is basically about being quiet in God's presence. My own usual practice is to begin by reading the passage from the Gospels that will be read that day in the Eucharist. I might go over it several times, as in the practice of *Lectio divina*. One advantage of this is that I don't start with myself, but with a voice from outside myself, God's Word. This is particularly significant when I am preoccupied or even worried—the Scriptures knock me off my chair, take me out of that little world, and set my feet in the large room of God and others. Inevitably it will probably lead, further along the line, to my current preoccupations. I have not turned from them, just opened the window. Whole libraries have been written on the practice of silent prayer in the monastic tradition, and it is not possible to say more on it here, apart from saying that for myself at least it is an absolute fountainhead, drinking at the deep sources of the Divine mystery, and being, as it were, set in motion, set on my feet and tuned in—looking into the face of Christ, which puts me profoundly on my mettle. It can be difficult to come away, but away we must, as 9 a.m. is around the corner, and the work of the day waiting to be done.

The day's work

What do nuns and monks do all day? In my own community, the tasks include:

- running the church building and making it ready for services,
- running the large library with the help of paid staff and volunteers,
- working in the kitchen, again with the staff who help us,
- the finance department (very complicated nowadays),
- working with and supporting our paid staff,
- the bookshop,
- the infirmary (looking after any infirm brothers, and seeing to the medical needs that are always coming up),
- looking after the extensive grounds with the help of a small team of paid helpers and volunteers,
- publishing our various publications, news sheets and journal,
- engaging with the world through the internet,
- live-streaming all our services,
- care of the internal running and the structure of a large and rambling building,
- some teaching in our theological college,
- being spiritual directors to hundreds of people,
- running the guest department (with rooms for a maximum of 75 guests),
- the archive,
- the laundry,
- care and training of novices,
- oversight and support of hundreds of Companions (friends of the community who follow a simple rule),
- and our Oblates and Associates (people who make a serious commitment to walking with us in their own way of life in the world),

- the Society of the Resurrection (similar to the Oblates, but open to men and women, and committed to being a community together, even though dispersed over various countries, by regular contact through the internet),
- organizing, leading or contributing to conferences and events, either at Mirfield or in other places,
- leading retreats,
- studying,
- taking part in the counsels of the wider Church such as the General Synod,
- a variety of ecumenical engagements,
- involvement in trail-blazing work for and with young people in Zimbabwe,
- attending numerous committees and councils of the community and college,
- cleaning,
- laying tables,
- washing up . . .

All of that will give an idea at least that after 9 a.m. each day there is no shortage of things to be done.

Special mention should be made of study. Every community needs to be mentally and spiritually nourished, and how that is done will differ. There is a need for spiritual reading to carry forward the journey of prayer, and for study of the Scriptures, and theological and other study, including seeking to know and understand contemporary society. Springs of life are also to be found in exploring other areas of interest of any kind whatsoever (we had one brother who was an international expert on beetles), as well as literature and the arts. The individual monk or nun has their own particular path of study, but corporate learning takes place too.

Midday

At midday, the community is summoned by bells to church again for a short Midday Office of a hymn and Psalms, followed in a different part of the church by the Eucharist. The Eucharist, as for all Christians, is a particular strong point in our worshipping life, day in and day out (more on this later). That is followed by lunch together, a meal at which we normally talk. We wait in the hall until a bell is rung and the person presiding (usually the Superior) leads the way into the refectory. We stand silently at our places waiting for everybody to get in, and after the Grace we sit to eat. Care is taken that everybody has what they need, that the food is passed around, and that any visitor is included in the conversation. At the end of the meal, all stand for another Grace, and then we face inwards to the central path between the tables while the presider walks out. We all help in clearing the tables, getting stuff onto trolleys and into the kitchen, where the brother who is washer-up and the washing-up machine are waiting.

Afternoon and evening

The afternoon is much like the morning, except that most brothers take brief recreation: a walk, or gardening, running, swimming or going to the gym. A cup of tea at 4 refreshes those who seek it, in a time of often lively conversation. We are back in church again at 6 p.m. for Evensong, much like Mattins except that even more of the service is sung. Then comes supper, a light meal eaten in silence while one brother reads out loud from a book, which can be of any suitable kind.

The final service of the day is Compline, similar to the Midday Office, but with the same Psalms every day of the year, followed by special prayers. By 9.35, now in Greater Silence, all are off to their rooms and ere long to bed.

Habits

There is a lot more that hasn't been mentioned here. I don't want to send the reader to sleep, but this sketches the main elements of the community's external praxis—what a fly on the wall might see. It varies for Sundays, saints' days and festivals, and also slightly on different days of the week, but this is the basic pattern in my community. This description of what you can see happening in the life of a monastic community needs now to go on to say something about the stage-set and costumes. To start with the latter, in most communities members wear a habit, a special form of dress derived from a long history, which may include slight variety within some communities, but on the whole everyone in the community wears the same thing. What we wear has the power to affect our frame of mind, and the "habit" is nothing less than a uniform fleshing out the identity of the community, the members as brothers and sisters on an equal plane, and evoking the liturgy with its own flowing robes. The habit breaks down borders of all sorts. A brother in our community can go straight from washing up the community's breakfast to preach at an impressive ordination in the cathedral in exactly the same clothes. Nowadays, however, some more active communities wear normal everyday clothes rather than a habit.

Buildings

Then there are the buildings. The Chapel will be a well-worn workplace: seeing it, being in it day by day, fixes its images in our minds so that it becomes inseparably woven up with all the prayer and people and the life. You cannot have a religious community without a chapel. There are communities without chapels who worship in their local church, but they are still likely to have a place in their house set apart for prayer. There is not a sharp division between the Chapel and the house of a community—the times of silence are in fact an extending of the climate of the Chapel into the house. The house needs certain standard items: a refectory for the common meals set out in a particular way, a kitchen (a special community place in itself), a room for meeting as a community, offices and workshops, and, somewhere buried away at the heart of the building, the cell of each brother or sister. This room isn't like a bedsit, a person's home, because the much larger monastery contains many items that would be part of anybody else's home. There are various things to learn about the cell, but one that will be noticeable, at least in my community, is that in the corridors where the brothers' rooms are, the silence is permanent. Open the door and go in, and you will see that no one needs more than a few books, because the community has a library. The other thing that may strike you is the simplicity—the room is not a nest, and has no need to be. There may be restricted hours when the radio can be on softly, but in general the room is silent.

Usually there will be a nice garden, and the less the community goes off the site, the more extensive the grounds are likely to be. In addition, the greater the hospitality offered by the community, the bigger the outdoor area needs to be, in order for all to find the space they are needing. Not everyone likes gardening, but we all flourish on contact with the earth and with nature. My community has a corporate gardening day once a month.

Behind what you see

Next we move on to things that might only be picked up by a fly on the wall that has a bit of nouse, things that don't simply count as visible activities in a series. For instance, the vows. Remember that in this chapter we are just trying to describe what happens, not yet concerning ourselves with underlying spiritual significance.

Vows

In my community, we make the three Benedictine vows of obedience, conversion of life and stability. Fundamental is *obedience*. What the fly on the wall will see is brothers or sisters (or both, depending on the nature of the community) working hard to submit themselves to one another in love, as St Paul puts it. This will be achieved with varying degrees of success—there will be moments of self-assertion, resistance or conflict, but there is something in the grain of the way people behave which gives a high priority to mutual submission and listening. The Superior is to be listened to in a particular way, being the focus of the unity of the community and in the place of Christ. The word "obedience" means listening, and concerns more than mere giving of orders to be carried out—in a community the Superior has to listen to all the members, and all the members seek to listen to each other—obedience flourishes in a circle of listening. If a member is asked to do something, by the Superior or by another member, then they respond in a spirit of listening. But the request itself will have been made in the same spirit—when you ask somebody to do something, you need to know them well enough to know whether they are capable of doing it. We shall explore this practice of listening further in Chapter 7, with its implications for parish life.

The vow of *stability* is seen in the way people stick at it: they remain with what is before them, without flitting from one thing to another. However tough or uncongenial any elements of the life may be, you stick with them, just as when, in drilling a borehole for a water supply, you carry on drilling on one spot. What the fly on the wall sees is a group of people doing their best to live with constancy at the offices, diligence in work, perseverance through all the difficulties, and feet seeking to be placed on the rock which is God. Things can go wrong and are never perfect, but the whole drift is perfectly visible to our fly. The vow of stability evolved in a situation where some people were tempted to play at being monks, while constantly drifting around from place to place, ending up as superficial dilettantes. In our world of today, where so much is constantly drifting around from one thing to the next, the Church is particularly called to be a pile driver, committing itself to some solid constancies through thick and thin without deflecting from them. Among them we can count Sunday attendance, Daily Prayer, commitments to helping our neighbour, faithfulness to commitments we have entered into, and sheer steadfastness. It is worth asking, in a parish, what the points of stability need to be, and what we have to give to people who feel adrift in one way or another in our unstable world. People can be affected by seeing that kind of constancy, as my community frequently hears from people who watch our streamed services.

Conversion of life is an unusual vow that does not mean what you think it might, although the process of conversion is part of it. The original Latin speaks of conversation rather than conversion, and this "conversation" is the whole of the life. The Latin writer Pliny once said the Eagle's conversation is in the mountains. In the Authorised Version of the Bible, Philippians 3:20 is rendered "our conversation is in heaven". So this vow refers to growing into the whole way of life, frame of mind and praxis of the community. It's about taking on board, and being taken into, a culture. It therefore refers to everything: the activities, the services, the timetable, attitudes, relationships and so on that are outlined in the whole of this chapter, the "conversation" of our life. All the vows pick up aspects of the gospel, and this particular one seems to have an acute message for the wider Church. Christ calls us to live one way of life, all of us as one, and this is threatened by the level of division and disagreement within the Church today. The vow of *conversatio* speaks of living one life together, in one culture, of diversity-in-unity, with a sense that this way of life is the domain of the Holy Spirit. There are no easy answers for the tensions in the Church today, with sometimes considerable differences between Christians living in their different boxes, but we need to work harder to be aware of each other and to seek a sufficient unity of the Church's culture. Christians go about their Christianity in very different ways, while the monastic practice of "Conversion/Conversation" is able to unfold the many layers of what it means to live in unity and treasure a common culture.

The vows are not a contract to certain particular things: they are a representative selection from a wider range of commitments. The life assumes for example the "evangelical counsels" of poverty, chastity, and the obedience already mentioned. *Chastity* refers to control of the passions and desires, but is specifically a marker that celibacy is a condition of the life. One origin of the word "monastic" is the Greek word *monos*, meaning "single". It enables community, but is also important for something referred to in the Scriptures as singleness of heart. It is visible that monks and nuns are celibate, and this belongs with the fact that they are a community. At the purely practical level, sexual activity here simply doesn't work. It is not honest, countering the public claim we are making, and it separates the person from the rest of the community, who are seeking to live the sacrifice of the single life together, and in a way it would undermine them. Hopefully the fly on the wall will see that this celibacy doesn't make people cold, or afraid to talk about sex, or repressed. There are today experimental ways in which married couples seek to be included in the life of a community, but they are always dependent on the primary monastic witness.[2]

Rowan Williams has said that "monastic practice . . . attempt[s] to return to the Gospel . . . The call that Jesus utters in the pages of the Gospels is undoubtedly a call into a community in which other kinds of human belonging together are cast into shadow . . . the simple natural affinities of the world around [family, nation, politics, language, and so on]".[3] Celibacy is a help in this direction, but we have to note, as so often we will in this book, that in the Gospels this is a call to everybody, not a specialism for nuns and monks. Religious communities live in conditions which help them flag it up, but every Christian is called to live in this way, putting Christ ahead of everything else that has a call upon us. The monastic ideal can perhaps prod all of us in this direction, to wrestle with the question of how the priority for Christ can really be lived in our lives.

With the notion of *poverty* we have to be careful. Those communities that live in prosperous Western countries cannot claim to be poor—that would be an insult to those who are truly poor. What we can aim at is simplicity of life and lack of possessions. Inevitably a community may hold many possessions corporately, but it has to continue to view and to use them as manifestations of its life. If they fail that test, they need to go. In my community, each brother buys the clothes he needs, and the community pays. Wherever possible we go first to charity shops. Care for appearances can be not very high on the agenda. The Superior of a

---

[2] For instance, the Community of Jesus on Cape Cod in the USA has many married couples with children.

[3] Rowan Williams: *Monastic Virtues and Ecumenical Hopes*, Address by Archbishop Rowan Williams, at *Monasticism and Ecumenism: a Conference*, San Gregorio Magno al Celio, 11 March 2012. <http://rowanwilliams. archbishopofcanterbury.org/articles.php/2385/monastic-virtues-and-ecumenical-hopes-archbishops-address-at-san-gregorio-magno.html>, accessed 16 October 2023.

well-known community was once invited to preach at a big occasion in St Paul's Cathedral but had difficulty getting past the verger on the door, who assumed from appearances that he was an eccentric man of the road.

We don't need to live and dress like that to take seriously in our own lives what the vow of poverty highlights: it is yet another aspect of the gospel that is for all Christians—living simply, having a care for the poor, not taking ourselves too seriously, living with generosity.

Talking together

The next thing to observe will be how communities talk together. The Superior brings all important matters to the meetings of Chapter, which in my and many other communities includes every professed member (those who have made their vows). You will not often find in these meetings the passionate defending of personal positions, statements that sit in judgement on another member, or the taking of strong individual stances, all of which are common in contemporary democracy. There will sometimes be differences of opinion and strong emotions, but the whole feel of it pulls in another direction, the common quest for the will of God, in the knowledge that we are all imperfect sinners. There will be difference, and discussion, but votes will be avoided, a show of hands only being asked for in certain cases: the commitment is to finding the common mind. Once decisions are made, all accept them even if some dislike them.

Rule

Every community has its rule. My own community had a rule composed in Victorian times; it remains a waymarker for us, but was too much of its time and has now taken a back seat, ceding place to a standard combination of the Rule of St Benedict (the inspirational document opening to us the wisdom of the tradition), a book of Constitutions (the actual rules for running a modern community), and a Customary (day-to-day rules that can be changed as needed). The community is fed and guided by its documents and by the wider corpus of writings in the monastic tradition, which is vast.

Social life

You may ask, where in all of this is there any corporate social life? An assumption from the outside might be that a community has a continuing, close life together. What you find is not really like the simple picture you might expect. If you think about it, the same can be said of any family. There may be a few intense focal moments, or times of close family "sharing" but, on the whole, family life is more diffused through various elements in the daily round. In a religious community, there is a multitude of opportunities for conversation: at some meals; within departmental teams; while attending committees, working groups, and Chapter meetings; at special occasions through the year; and during the practice of "recreation". The regularity of recreation varies from community to community, but it is a time for a mug or a glass of something with an informal time together which may include a special contribution, such as someone reporting on an event they have been away for.

It is probably true to say that communities are on a journey of discovery in this area of community life. To put it briefly, in the old days there was more of an expectation that you put your head down and got on with it. The world, however, has changed and continues to change, and there are now higher expectations as to what counts as authentic relating, as opposed to avoidance, and what it means to be human beings together. It is now not uncommon for communities to draw on the help of professional facilitators to work on that, and this has been true of my own community to our huge benefit. In that area there is an element of "watch this space", just as many times throughout the history of monastic life communities have recognized the need to adjust to the times. That, in fact, is what we are—ordinary people of our times. Visitors can come expecting people to be different—it is difficult to say what they expect, but it is usually something to do with pious conversation and an enclosed religious world; and so they are often surprised to discover that we are ordinary people who talk about the same things in the same kind of way as them, and can be as savvy about the world as anybody else. A closer look will also reveal that we are a bit odd. There may be occasions, for instance, when we go to speak in a parish and are lodged with a family—it can be difficult to live with the bustle, activities, TV, kids, dogs and pop music, and rather odd of us to disappear to our room for long periods, which we can find ourselves doing.

What the fly on the wall has seen in this chapter is a way of life that is distinctive. A break from it, as in holidays, can be not only refreshing but essential: but the community and its life become so much part of the stuff of which we are made as to be with us always.

It's now time to try and get a little below the surface of this life with its strange activities, and we will find ourselves discovering things that are just as applicable to ordinary Christians in the parish. Some of these things have been lost in parish life only relatively recently, sometimes with a loss so drastic that religious communities can seem today like pools in a dried-up riverbed, at which people come in numbers to drink. The modern world brings problems for religious communities too, however, and the truth of the matter is that monastery and parish and secular world all have much to give each other.

3

Things, people, practices

One aspect of the sample day in the last chapter that may strike you is the practices—in worship, at meals, in the ways we relate to each other—and here is something that speaks directly to everyone in the modern world in a way we will probably not expect. I can only illustrate it by telling another story. In my teenage visit to the friary at Alnmouth, I got to know Brother Harold, who later went on to found a hermitage on a remote Northumberland hill called Shepherds Law. I used to go there now and again to see him. The services in the chapel involved standing together at a big lectern-cum-bookcase in a dim chapel full of icons and other items. As a visitor, you sang the services together with him from the one book on the lectern, which would be changed for other books from the shelf as we went along. Psalms, canticles, readings, candles, icons, silences, bowing, sitting, standing, a very bodily way of worshipping, and happening six times a day. At a particular moment during one of these offices, as a book was being changed, a penny dropped—I had a revelation. I suddenly saw that my faltering personal faith was not all I depended on—these practices were a bridge to God, exercising my whole being, body and soul, sight, hearing, touch, sense of place. I had always found the offices beneficial, but at that moment I first saw the point of just getting on and doing it.

Leave it to your body

In this chapter, I want to try and explain what I mean about a penny dropping for me at that moment, and I will start in an unusual place—a dance floor on a Friday night in the 1950s. Victor Silvester's band strikes up and couples start to glide around the room, generally looking beyond each other. One thing is certain—they are not looking at their feet. Without looking to check, they nimbly step around each other with graceful deftness. Some talk quietly as they dance, or just enjoy it all vacantly. Are they thinking, "Now I put my right foot here, now my left foot there, now we turn, and now he puts his foot there . . . ?" Surely not. The dancing is not being done by their brains—it's taken care of by the feet and legs. When these nice people were learning the steps, they *had* to use their brains, certainly, but gradually a point came where it could be left to the feet. The conscious operation of the brain drops out, muscular memory takes over and the brain can get on with other things: affectionate conversation, anxious thoughts about the shopping, the need to find another job; the feet down below are deftly getting on with their expert work, the body sways and bends naturally, the space is instinctively mapped. To think about each step and bodily movement as you do it would cause you to stumble or tread on your partner's toes. It is the same with touch-typing, playing the piano, and many other skills in life. The mind has to get out of the way and let the body do the running. Concentrating on the actions can cause you to stumble. Think of any amount of things we do each day—walking, breathing, talking, going to sleep—done without thinking.

In recent years, research has revealed that many complex things we do originate more from the physical body than the mind. Often the brain seems to be left completely out of the picture. In body language for instance, we can betray our inner state quite unawares: the obsessive swinging of a foot, the uneasy look of our eyes. As I sit writing at my desk, someone knocks on the door. I bid them come in and greet them—I am sure my deliberate smile makes them feel at home, but in my face they see traces of irritation. Our bodies send out more information than we realize. The monastic day described in Chapter 2 partly works in just this way, and it teaches us something about ourselves, if we would just stop to consider it.

Hidden depths

In one psychological study, thinking about the *future* caused participants to lean slightly forwards, while thinking about the *past* caused them to lean slightly backwards.[4] In another study, participants holding warm cups of coffee were more likely to judge someone trustworthy than those holding cups of cold coffee.[5] Physical illness can cause depression; depression can be a source of physical illness; people who are happy tend to stand tall and perky; sadness can make us droop. We are discovering the myriad ways our minds and bodies are interconnected. We used to think of the mind as the superior part of our being, the seat of our thinking, deciding, assessing and emotions, while the body belongs to a lower level, dealing with practical necessities under the command of the mind. We are discovering that is not quite true. I was recently struck by an illustration in a magazine: it showed a huge robot a firm had constructed, bigger than a house. In place of its head was a driver's cab, and in the cab was a real man pulling levers, driving the robot. That's how we think of our inner selves, the little chap driving our body; but to illustrate our human being more accurately, the cab in the head of the huge robot needs to be got rid of, and replaced by a huge soul that fills the whole robot. This soul is often in the feet, the fingertips, the whole body. Just think of yourself as living within your entire body.

There is another aspect of this to do with our unconscious mind. If you look at the variety of objects around you in your living room, they carry memories, associations, needs, evocations of other places, dormant, waiting to be awoken. Still more lies inside the closed photograph

---

[4] Samuel McNerney, *A Brief Guide to Embodied Cognition: Why You Are Not Your Brain*, Scientific American Guest Blog, November 4, 2011. <https://blogs.scientificamerican.com/guest-blog/a-brief-guide-to-embodied-cognition-why-you-are-not-your-brain/>, accessed 16 October 2023.

[5] McNerney, *A Brief Guide to Embodied Cognition*.

albums, videos, collections of letters, and, even much more, the people we live with. Habit makes us routinely unconscious of the richness we are swimming in at home. One person who blazed a trail in recognizing this was Maurice Merleau-Ponty, a French philosopher who died in 1961. He says that what we encounter visibly in people and things is "the surface of an inexhaustible depth".[6] Every person I see on the bus is the surface of an inexhaustible depth. We have many layers in us receding further and further down inside us, beyond our sight—a tacit world that is always there, dormant, and only bubbles up when prodded. Photos, music, names of people we have known, can wake up things in us that were asleep. What this teaches us is that there is a two-way connection between these things and my hidden layers. I invest things and people with memories, and they awaken memories in me. Often they have been the instruments for laying down the memories in me. The first time I hear a piece of music it is simply new and unknown. The second time, there is a touch of familiarity. In subsequent hearings, it becomes more and more a part of me, so that I can be singing some parts of it in my head even before the music gets there. What is less easy to register is what the music is doing to me. It affects my pulse, my breathing, my sense of wellbeing, it can induce a mood. I can't see that at all so well.

Practices

This has implications for the Christian life. One thing I have been becoming increasingly aware of over my almost 40 years in monastic life is perhaps surprising: you think of monastic life as an interior journey in a life of contemplation. It is certainly that, but I have become more and more aware of the *objectivity* of the life too. It is rich in practices, apparently religious, all mixed up with practical ones: worshipping in church several times every day, washing up for many people, praying on your own, living in community, staying in one place without coming and going as you want, learning how to get on with people who can be

---

6   Maurice Merleau-Ponty, *The Visible and the Invisible* (Evanston, IL: Northwestern University Press, 1964), p. 143.

difficult or uncongenial, looking after many guests, running the finances, practising obedience, and so on—a cornucopia of *practices* of every kind, in which each of us is honed, tuned, brought up against God, against humanity, and against ourselves and, in short, over many years, we are gradually changed. Private prayer and meditation, and the personal journey of the heart, are an essential part of this, but not the only part. In my community, we have a Chapter meeting once a week, and one of the things we do in this meeting is to go round confessing ways we have failed to do what is required of us by our life—in the keeping of silences, time spent in prayer, breaking of the library rule and so on. Many communities have abandoned this practice, but we still find it a good thing to do. Not only is it a way of apologizing to each other for failures which leave others to pick up the tab, but the effect over the years of this usually pretty routine practice is to instil some important things about being brothers/sisters together: it reminds us every week of the things we are committed to, and helps sustain an innate sense of what we are about in the sight of God. It has its humorous moments—on one occasion a few years ago a brother said, "I have broken the silence of the kitchen and 20 plates, and caused another brother to speak." It can also be one of those indicators to each other of how we are, what life is like for us at the moment. That is just one example of a practice that might be thought to be formalistic and without depth.

George Lindbeck was an American Lutheran scholar who is particularly remembered for his book *The Nature of Doctrine*, published in 1984. He makes no reference to monastic life, but what he says about Christian living is very relevant here. He says that "to become religious . . . is to interiorize a set of skills by practice and training".[7] We sit under the practices, as it were—we trust them—and through that perseverance we tend to grow in spiritual skills, quite unawares. Lindbeck speaks of the development of intuitive skills and "nouse". He says, "Interiorized skill, the skill of the saint, manifests itself in an ability to discriminate 'intuitively' . . . between [what is] authentic [and] inauthentic." St Benedict's Rule in a similar way says surprisingly little about personal

---

[7] George Lindbeck, *The Nature of Doctrine* (Louisville, KY: Westminster/John Knox Press, 1984), p. 35.

prayer or the spiritual life—he is more interested in introducing us to the practical living, in all its details, of a way of life in which these things can germinate. In Lindbeck's words, "First come the objectivities of the religion, its language, doctrines, liturgies and modes of action, and it is through these that passions are shaped into various kinds of what is called religious experience."[8] Lindbeck's picture of the *practices* of Christian life developing "skills" in us puts very well what I have been saying about the way monastic life forms its members' frame of mind over the years.

The effect of practices is everywhere

Over the last 30 or more years, researchers have been exploring these effects of outward practice, the connection of the physical world with things deep within us. Once you see it, you then find it everywhere you look. Think of life in a family. How much of it is deep personal engagement all the time? Isn't a large part of it woven through the things that go on in the home? The things you do together—fun things, humdrum ones, things that cause damage and hurt, practical actions—they all contribute to laying down a deep stratum within us that is just—simply—there. When you are out and about doing things away from home, you don't keep consciously trying to think of the family—it's just there as part of your makeup. In monastic life, in a similar way, all the practices that make up the life become more and more like the milk mingling in a cup of tea, a suffusing in you of skills for living, an unselfconscious walking with God's people in all areas of your life. What I see in the monastery of our Christian practices shaping our spirituality, Lindbeck thinks can be the case for Christians in ordinary life; it is something that has been the case in the past and needs to be recovered.

He shows that there used to be a time when being Christian required laying great emphasis on accepting propositions—simply saying "yes" to teachings. People today have no faith in that: on its own it is dead and unconvincing. Instead there is nowadays a great reliance on personal feelings and personal response. This is a great step forward, but in the end

---

[8]   Lindbeck, *The Nature of Doctrine*, p. 39.

it is not enough, because my personal life is hopelessly depleted without other people. Following God can't simply be personal—the first thing Jesus did was to gather together a group, and he encouraged faith within the group, not a faith to be lived in private corners. Where you will find real life and creativity going on you have a chemistry between persons, each of them personally animated and living their individual journey, but bringing it together with others.

So religion as teachings you have to accept is now out, but the purely private, personal approach is now beginning to show its weaknesses too, and another, third way is now emerging—or I should say re-emerging, for it is very ancient, and thoroughly rooted in the New Testament; this is the holistic approach to following Christ we are starting to outline. It will be one of the major themes of this book.

We are in for a big change

Such an approach goes against the grain of all our inherited assumptions about faith and about prayer. We inherit a great emphasis on the personal pilgrimage of each individual in a private relationship with God. For us, it has to be authentic for me-in-my-privacy. This emphasis on personal faith, however, is very recent. We see beginnings of it in the later Middle Ages, but it was only in the latter part of the seventeenth century that people suddenly started developing a new sense of interiority that had far-reaching implications for religion: it led to a growing emphasis on our interior life, our subjectivity. Owen Barfield says, "The consciousness of 'myself' and the distinction between [that] and all other selves . . . the external world . . . is such an obvious and early fact of experience to every one of us, such a fundamental starting point of our life as conscious beings, that it really requires a sort of training of the imagination to be able to conceive of any different kind of consciousness. Yet . . . this form of ['personal'] experience . . . is quite a recent achievement of the human spirit."[9] So we see the beginnings of talk about "personal faith". We have lived for two or three centuries now in this climate, and what it has left us

---

9   Owen Barfield, *History in English Words* (London: Faber, 1964), p. 164.

with is a range of deep assumptions that we think are self-evident. Most of all, we think it self-evident that religious faith should start and finish with my personal experience and convictions. I hope to show why this can't normally be the case. This over-emphasis on the personal is one reason why many people today struggle with prayer and with faith—they are trying to do something that is not natural. Certainly, personal faith is an essential element in the New Testament—what we are saying is that this absolute emphasis on it is not to be found there.

We assume that the heart of being Christian is that each of us should have a living personal relationship with God, and that prayer should first of all be a personal journey in that relationship, something pursued with our inner being, our minds and souls. In some ways, development of this assumption marked an advance in Christian living. The emphasis on a personal relationship has grown hand in hand with our gradual growth in the capacity for self-reflection. More people are self-reflective today than would have been common in the seventeenth century. (I put it that way because some of us even today are of course less sensitive and self-reflective than others!) We look at ourselves, and we consider how we are, how we behave, and we try to learn and adjust as may be needed. So we might say something to someone, but think afterwards, "I hope I didn't come over as too bossy." We are more given to self-reflection than people were in earlier centuries. As we go back in time, people tend to be less self-sensitive. There have been great gains from our growth in the capacity for inner reflection; self-knowledge and openness to change can only be a sign of the gospel at work. The problem I am trying to highlight is that this self-reference has somehow got out of proportion when it comes to prayer and the life of faith. The deeply personal approach to faith has downgraded the body and the *practical*. This notion of faith being utterly personal has led us astray because we have *enthroned* it, rather than letting it have its proper place with other things on the ladder.

Imperatives in arms and legs

Pierre Bourdieu, another philosopher (again French), has delved into this ignored fact about us. For him, *belief* is a state of the body, a rapport between bodily habits and the surrounding world of human culture to which these habits are attuned. In childhood, the child's body leads the child's mind. So you learn by bumping into things, or putting them in your mouth. Out of these experiences the child develops mental habits. A lot of these habits then continue to live in our limbs—you begin instinctually to avoid things that stick out. Bourdieu says that "adapting a phrase of Proust's, one might say that arms and legs are full of numb imperatives"[10]—like the feet of ballroom dancers. Belief, therefore, is not just something that lives in our head—it is enacted, sensed, swum in, by our bodies. Think of the powerful effect Communion can have, and the distress that can be caused if people are denied Communion.

If the child's body learns by bumping into things, what it has learned then works the other way. Physical practices can re-awaken habitual feelings that lie dormant within us. For instance, at a funeral in a traditional society the familiar texts, music and practices trigger emotions and tears because they are so well known; they play out a symphony of human feeling and experience, evocative of community, human solidarity and, simply, things deep and indescribable. Our society has lost most of its deep funeral practices—what is left is debris like our smartly if strangely dressed undertakers and their formal behaviour. That often leaves us with emotional poverty and inarticulacy, unhealed wounds and, sometimes, illness, because our bodies, sight, hearing etc. have nothing to do and they long to have something to do.

A healthy repertoire of practices can help us to live healthily with our emotions. But they can do more: they can instil things in us that have not been there. William Desmond has written:

> Act in an angry way, and the anger comes, act in a loving way
> and the loving can come, act in a gentle way, and consideration

---

[10] Pierre Bourdieu, *The Logic of Practice* (Stanford, CA: Stanford University Press, 1990), p. 68.

comes. Pascal made the point that by taking holy water, even if one does not believe, the action will seed something that communicates of belief. Kneel and prayer may come.[11]

It is in this kind of way that the practices of monastic life have a potential to convert the people who live in religious communities. This suggests that what applies to them applies to everybody. The practices of Christianity have a potential to convert all of us.

Being Christian today

What might these thoughts have to say to us today? An obituary of a well-known anthropologist a few years ago quoted him as saying religions are not concerned with belief, but with practice. We might be surprised at that. But if you look at the conversion stories in the New Testament, you may be surprised by how few people ask, "What must I believe?" The findings of anthropologists are pretty clear that religion in human history has followed this unexpected path: it started with people doing things, practising certain things in a very practical way; gradually it moved on to what they felt, to an emotional involvement; and in the longer term they began to tease this out in beliefs about what they were doing. The order of things is practice, then engagement, then belief, a classic religious trio. In the Western culture that we have inherited, there is an expectation that belief should come first. This expectation is about being able to screw up within ourselves an ability to believe, saying to ourselves, "Can I believe that? . . . I'll try." Then we often end up saying, "I don't see how I can believe that." There have always been people who have come to faith through embracing beliefs, but they are the exception—we come to God through intercourse with God through the means God gives. God addresses us, encounters us, and then God leads us to reflect on that experience and to find ways of putting it into words. In that process, we

---

[11]   William Desmond, quoted in Dennis Vanden Auweele, "Sacredness and aesthetics: Kearney and Desmond on prayer", *Modern Theology* 37:1 (2021), p. 21.

draw on all that has been done by people who have gone before us, and so we find ourselves exploring the treasure-house of Christian doctrine. But you can't digest the doctrine until you have lived the actual reality that it attempts to capture. The engagement comes first, and this leads to the articulation and digesting of beliefs. In the Gospels, it is the encounter with Jesus that transforms. What he said made a lot of sense to many people, but his teachings and his person are one whole bundle—you can't separate off the teachings and get the full message. Many non-believers, after all, admire Jesus' teaching without it bringing them to an encounter with God.

How today can we come to an encounter with God? You may have noticed that in talking about Jesus I have only mentioned engagement leading to belief: there is the third bit of our anthropologists' trio that precedes both of them: practices. According to the Gospels, what leads to engagement with Jesus is a hurly-burly of things going on: meetings, baptisms, verbal exchanges, organizing in groups, times of prayer, meals together, so many meals, journeyings, practical events such as healings, the Transfiguration, a hurly-burly which Mark's Gospel depicts as pretty breathless. When they ask him about prayer, Jesus gives them the Lord's Prayer to repeat. When he wants to leave them with something fundamental, he gives them the Eucharist. Then at the heart of the faith lie things that are *done*: Christ's Passion, crucifixion, God raising Christ from the dead, the coming of the Holy Spirit. Things are done, then engagement follows; and then begins the long process of articulating our belief about it all.

Practising practices today

We need to get the trio in the right proportion: action, engagement, belief. We are hot on the personal engagement bit, often with mixed results through having enthroned it. We are also hot on belief, assuming that this has to be the starting point for experiencing the encounter with God. This is not quite right, and so we need here to take a serious look at our practices. We need to find out—and the challenge is not easy—how we can become practically and physically strong again, in our own way, for our own time; strong in the kind of actions and practices which before modern times were common everywhere. In pre-modern societies, life was full of practices you simply did, in both secular and religious life. Eamon Duffy's book *The Stripping of the Altars* gives a good picture of this for the Middle Ages in Britain. He describes a whole array of medieval prayer practices, some of which we will recognize as still being practised today, or having been rediscovered, and some that seem to belong more to the past—they reflect a particular culture very different from ours, but if we make allowances for that, the list gives us some idea of what we are talking about. Some of them are difficult to disentangle from the public liturgy of the Church, because in fact there is not a hard-and-fast boundary between the two. Private prayer and public prayer are two aspects of one thing. Duffy's catalogue includes:

- Attending the daily offices in the parish church (at least six were available every day),
- Saying or singing little offices alone or in the home,
- Rhymed offices,
- Prayers when starting different things in the day, such as meals or going to bed,
- Making the sign of the cross,
- Using postures: standing, sitting, kneeling, prostrating, bodily movements,
- Lighting candles,
- Belonging to guilds that maintained lamps and other supplies for the church building,
- Praying to Saints,
- Saying the Rosary or Paternoster Beads,
- Repeating prayers while counting on the fingers,
- Praying aloud,
- Holding things while praying,
- The Lord's Prayer, Hail Mary and Creed, a trio often said or sung together,
- Saying prayers for particular things: petition and intercession,
- Praying for the departed,
- Visiting graves,

- Using books of prayers (if you were literate),
- Going in the church building, or praying at wayside crosses or shrines,
- Taking part in processions and special events,
- Pilgrimage,
- Having the parish clerk bless things regularly with Holy Water.

Many practices were open to abuse or misinterpretation, but for most people they were a strong framework for real Christian prayer. We could not resurrect all of them even if we wanted to—we live in a very different culture. There are things we can learn from the list, but the emphasis needs to be on exploring what God is calling us to today in our own time.

If we want to ask what kind of Christian practices will work for us today, there is something we need to have clear in our minds: many practices in secular life require some preliminary know-how. It's like going swimming in the open air in cold weather. There are things you need to know that you might not have thought of, such as getting in cold water gradually, not quickly; not staying in it so long that the cold affects your brain unawares; covering up immediately afterwards with plenty of insulation; drinking a hot drink; not doing some things that might seem obvious, like an immediate hot shower, and so on. That is largely medical know-how. If someone is teaching you to sing, there are counter-intuitive things that need to become habits: learning how to breathe properly, not raising your shoulders when you take deep breaths, knowing when to raise your eyebrows, how to open your mouth in strange shapes, how to stand. There is a similar know-how for Christian practices of prayer and the Christian journey, and in the next two chapters we will look at two important ones, without which we are likely to go off on a goose chase. With them, we can hope to work on a solid and well-tested foundation.

4

Community and communion

We are exploring a surprising thought: that we today are too quick to assume faith should be founded on deep, interior personal engagement, and that in order to engage with Christ we think we need to be convinced by some beliefs first. We feel we need to experience something in ourselves if we are going to start on the Christian journey. In these expectations, we have been saddled with a misunderstanding, coming from how our society has developed over recent centuries. Compared with the Gospels, and even with our own daily lives, these assumptions are unrealistic, and it is not surprising as a result that many people struggle with belief and with prayer. We have seen that, just as in daily life, any relationship with God is likely to start by doing things; and we have talked about the place of the body in prayer, and of the role of actions and practices. It would be natural now to go on to think about what practices could be good for us in our own day, but before we do that we need to look at two other things. The first of these is community.

Community

Community is a buzzword nowadays: it is largely felt to be a good thing, good for people, good in itself. We don't always know how to find community and can complain there isn't enough of it. However, when there is the possibility of closer involvement in a community we hold back—what limitations will it impose on me, how will it trim my sails, what will I have to put up with from other people? We are wary today of committing ourselves, and this is something well known to religious communities, where individuals can come and enquire but find it difficult to take the plunge. When I go wild-water swimming in cold weather, I get there, and then think again and wish I hadn't come. I stand at the edge of this high-up reservoir in the Yorkshire hills: "No, George," I say to myself, "you can't get in that." Then I go backwards and forwards at the edge, unable to get in. I remind myself of how frustrated I will feel when I get home, having traipsed all the way there and done nothing. Only such calculations get me in it. After the first unspeakable ten seconds, sheer gloriousness takes over, and I wonder, "What was all the fuss about?" That is how we are when faced with many forms of commitment today, not least community. And yet we are social animals: we flourish in life with others. Loneliness and isolation are typically modern problems since at least the 1960s, with disintegration of the extended family and the widespread disappearance of intermediate groups, a story tellingly told in Robert Putnam's book *Bowling Alone*: neighbourhood spirit, clubs and friendly societies, churches and other social groups have shrunk or disappeared with little to replace them. This gives expansion room to darker aspects of community. Social media's groups and groupings sometimes bear characteristics of community, but are always pale imitations, and often forums for desires and passions out of balance.

Herd instincts

We human beings meanwhile have an inbuilt herd instinct, which is an inescapable part of us. It is with us still, even today, passionately among football fans, nationally in something like Brexit, and in our own lives if a group we belong to is challenged. When my community planned to reorder its monastic church, this stirred some vocal opposition, climaxing in a court case. Not only did we spring to our defence, but we were quick to respond emotionally to what were perceived as attacks—it was difficult not to slip into us-and-them passions, to get ourselves on a battle footing. We kept our heads on the whole, but the "us-and-them" genie comes easily out of the bottle: such instincts are deep inside us, automatically coming into play when circumstances stir them up.

The herd instinct, with its powerful us-and-them emotions, comes up out of our depths; these days it seems as though it can rise up out of nowhere. Once a threat is over, the "herd" once united by those feelings can dissolve as quickly as it came together, and there is precious little community to provide conditions for the moderation of the feelings some people continue to carry, as used to happen in the past.

Another aspect of the herd instinct that is still with us, and is different from a sense of community, is the urge to conform, where, for example, the latest style of clothing is a must-have. This lives in strange company with individualism, and shouts at us every day in many ways. Many of us seek to be unique individuals in our appearance, while we feel the need to adopt practices of society or a group within it at the same time.

Used aright, our herd instincts have real potential for good, but for that they need to have their windows open. It can be great to be patriotic, it can be good to have a sense of loyalty to a trade union, or passion for our team in a cricket match, but any of those can go wrong. The enjoyment and fulfilment provided by football can go wrong if opposing fans start knifing each other. Social media have given free rein to these herd instincts, and to instincts for hunting a victim. But we need go no further than an innocent church meeting to find the red line being crossed, when people angrily defend their positions and fail to make the effort to try and see things from the other's point of view. When a fall-out is reported in the church press, or someone in authority has put everyone's backs up, we know the herd instinct is around.

Discussion with respect

St Benedict has various things to say to all of this. In his time, leadership tended to be autocratic. There was a strong tendency in leaders to assume their opinions were right and others wrong, something not unfamiliar today, but more widespread and automatic in the sixth century. In his time, authority meant power, which could often be as arbitrary as it wanted. Benedict moved against that, introducing something that went completely contrary to such a culture. In Chapter 3 of his Rule, he says that on important matters the Abbot has to consult the brethren. This was nothing new—what is new is the way Benedict treats it. The Abbot still makes the final decision, but he has to listen to everyone carefully.

Everyone has to be called to the meeting, even the youngest and newest recruits. Benedict surprisingly says the Lord often reveals what is better to the younger; this was in a culture where age counted for wisdom—the older you are, the more clout you have in decision-making. Reading between the lines we can see Benedict targeting older people who simply assumed they were right, and whose motto might be "this is the way we have always done it". He sought to break through all of that. The next verse (v. 4) is just as interesting: the brothers, for their part, are to express their opinions with all humility, and not presume to defend their own views obstinately. The monks are to listen to one another with complete openness. In Chapter 72, Benedict says:

> This . . . is the good zeal which monks must foster with fervent love: they should each try to be the first to show respect to the other (Romans 12:10), supporting with the greatest patience one another's weaknesses of body or behaviour, and earnestly competing in obedience to one another. No one is to pursue what he judges better for himself, but instead, what he judges better for someone else.

This spirit runs through the whole of Benedict's key Chapter 7 on humility: summing it up, in verse 62 he says, "The twelfth step of humility is that a monk always manifests humility in his bearing no less than in his heart, so that it is obvious." Earlier in the chapter he says, "Strive to be the first to honour one another." When therefore it comes to discussion in a meeting of the community, the spirit of the meeting is one of listening—of putting listening before speaking, and being realistic about the relative value of our own opinions. This theme of humility is fundamental to Benedict, and it plays out in many other ways. One is that we should never judge one another—we need to spend a lifetime learning that one. We need to have patience with other people's weaknesses and we need in fact simply to continue learning to love. Benedict here is talking about one of the fundamental building blocks of community.

Mutual respect in the modern world

When we look at modern life, we see a world that has known much of this but is now going backwards. People shout past each other, jumping up and down in defence of their own private opinions. It is there in politics, in the world of work, and in the Church. Christians today need the spirit of the gospel, not least as it is distilled in St Benedict. To take one of the most clamorous examples of this strident self-righteousness, we could look at the American presidential election of 2016. We are all familiar with Donald Trump's approach to the discussion of important things. Whatever else you may say about it, it is light years away from Benedict's approach. After the 2016 election, an organization grew up known as *Braver Angels*. James Wiseman, Abbot of a monastery in Washington DC, has written of this:

> [It began] in the town of South Lebanon, Ohio, in the aftermath of the hotly contested presidential election of 2016. About twenty . . . residents having very different political persuasions—some had voted for Donald Trump, others had . . . avidly wanted Hillary Clinton to win—came together over a weekend in December of that year . . . . The aim was simply to help the people who attended—about ten on each side of the political divide—come to a better understanding of their differences as well as to find any points of common ground. From that modest start in a small town in Ohio the organization has by now become national, with regular workshops, podcasts, and training sessions. At times its leaders have brought together politicians from red and blue states, at other times advocates of abortion rights alongside persons who want the procedure banned or at least severely limited, and at still other times persons who want to talk about race or environmental issues in an inquisitive, non-judgmental way. [It was named] Braver Angels because it was . . . realized that genuine *courage* was needed to pursue what Lincoln in his Second Inaugural had called a more perfect union, "with malice towards none, with charity for all, with firmness in the right". A fifty-minute documentary about the organization entitled *Braver*

Angels: Reuniting America is available on YouTube ... the film shows eight Democrat-leaning voters and seven Republican-leaning voters "moving through a Braver Angels ... workshop, from initial scepticism to more profound understanding and empathy" and so providing "an inside look at how a Democratic voter went from threatening to cut off relationships with Trump voters to becoming dear friends with one—and how a Republican voter moved from disdaining progressives to taking co-leadership with one in a movement that now spans the country".[12]

This way of relating to one another cannot simply be turned on—it has to be worked at all the time. Benedict himself will have been well aware that monastic communities need to continually remind themselves of these things. Monasteries cannot be held up as shining examples. They have their own bust-ups and conflicts where the gospel principles get damaged. Some communities, as I have already said, now make use of secular professional facilitators to help keep the community's members to the task. Humans being what they are, sustaining this approach to dialogue and decision-making is like maintaining the dykes in Holland. You have to work at it constantly with patience and with a will to remain aware of the presence of God. The fundamental principle of the meetings of a religious community is that its task is not to debate all opinions to see which one wins. It is there to discern the will of God. That is not a monastic speciality—it is a principle for all who seek to live by the gospel.

The Church

Herd instincts and us-and-them relating were at the top of the agenda in Jesus' ministry, and he was revolutionary in the way he tackled them. He put before people not a plan for constructing an ideal society, but something more intriguing—he took our primordial herd instincts, our capacity for team spirit, our hard-wiring for community, and

---

[12] James Wiseman, "Saint Benedict and the Raven", *American Benedictine Review* 73:3 (2022), p. 242.

transformed them into potentially their truest manifestation. This new thing is the divine society of the Church. Where the Church is living according to God's will, it transforms our herd instincts into a higher form of belonging. Feeling proud of our country always comes at the cost of how we see other countries; pride in the Church, however, is possible without any dismissing of anyone else. Christianity takes our instincts and passions and is able to use them by transforming them.

We have been thinking about the place of Christian practices in our lives, and we can now say that one piece of know-how that needs to be there when we go about Christian practices has to do with the Church. Just as a wild-water swimmer needs to know best practice, so Christians need to know best practice about prayer, and part of that is the Church. Some people say you can't talk about the Church today, particularly with our very secular younger generation, for whom the word "church" is off-putting or even toxic. The covering-up of abuse scandals, infights over women's ordination, perceived dog-in-manger attitudes over sexual ethics, and other publicity coming over negatively to the wider public, leave some people even within the Church saying the notion of "the Church" has to be put in its place. The Church as an institution, in this view, is too fallible for us to be able to trust it much. This goes back a few years. In the 1960s, a questioning of conventions and institutions included the Church, and carried with it a new recognition of the presence of Christ in our basic humanity and our human life. The institutional Church seemed cut off, a damper on real life. The Church had done things wrongly, made terrible mistakes, hurt and damaged people. It was now to be put in its place, subject to the free and joyful spirit of the gospel, lived in a *real* way in the midst of real everyday life.

The Church as iceberg

Many of the criticisms were justly aimed, but they were also ill judged, in assuming the Church to be a purely human, administrative institution. This ill judgement is still with us, particularly among churches of the Reformation. One example would be words from a celebrant of the Eucharist immediately before Communion, along the lines of: "Draw near and receive this sacrament, which is not a sacrament of the Church, but of Christ." According to this view, "Church" refers solely to the human institution, understood as having been set up by human beings, planned and run by them.

It is true that the institutional Church routinely makes a mess of things, and has done so ever since the evidence of it in the letters of St Paul, but it is at the same time a source of immense good in the world. Were it to disappear, the humanitarian toll would be incalculable. And in addition, as with icebergs, behind or underneath the visible there is a great invisible. The contemporary relativizing of the term "Church" simply refers to the visible. We cannot read the New Testament and find there such a picture of suspicion of the Church, of a great ditch between the Church and Christ. Paul Minear has identified 96 separate images of the Church in the New Testament; the richness of the language speaks of it as a mystery, desired and called forth by God for God's purposes, and sustained by him. Particularly in the Pauline and Johannine writings we find a powerful array of metaphors about it. You do not use metaphors at this level to talk about something equivalent to a gas company or a trade union. Minear has written of the New Testament that "behind the [96] images we sense a corporate awareness of a majesty that was at once heavenly and earthly".[13] So the earthly institution of the Church is in some ways in a mess and always has been, but without the rest of the iceberg, the "majesty" of the Church visible and invisible, the New Testament is contradicted.

In order to gain a sense of this majesty, we might think of the crashed meteorite that recently made a mess on someone's front drive. For them it would be easy to associate meteorites with mess, and to want simply to sweep it up. When, however, we look up at the sky at night we see the meteorite's awesome origin in a wonderful and breathtaking splendour— the stars and planets from which it has come. The meteorite that hit the drive is of great interest to scientists in helping them learn about the wider universe. The organization of the Church, and all the messes it seems to make on people's front drives, at the same time speaks with

---

[13]   Paul Minear, *Images of the Church in the New Testament* (Cambridge: Lutterworth Press, 1961), p. 224.

eloquence of something that won't fit neatly into our simple categories of good and bad. We can't separate the mess from the holiness—we learn this repeatedly not only in Jesus' gospel but in the Old Testament too, especially in the Psalms. God is there waiting for us in the bad bits as well as the good. In a field full of gold, we dig for gold not only where the gold is obvious, but also in the cow-muck. That is the picture the Scriptures give us, and so while wariness in relation to the Church is understandable—we should of course expect sometimes to be on our guard with relation to Church authorities—we are encouraged to look in the very mess itself for God's presence, as well as beyond, to the essential mystery of it, a throng of people living and departed, with Christ as their head, one Communion in the divine love.

How is the Church holy?

In just the same way, the life of religious communities cannot be reduced simply to the people who are at present living it—there is something bigger than them, which has a life of its own, and seems to do its stuff despite them sometimes.. The Church is a divine society which carries forward God's purposes often in curious contradiction to its members and those who run it. This principle is there in Article 26 of the 39 Articles in the Book of Common Prayer, where we are told the effectiveness of the sacraments does not depend on the character of the person celebrating them. They are bigger than that person.

The objection might be made that such a picture of the Church is Platonic, imagining an invisible reality beyond our sight, an ideal version of something that down here is imperfect. One difference from Plato, however, is that this ideal reality is not simply "up there" in heaven—it is down here and manifests itself physically. If Jesus has taken our herd instincts and brought them to their truest manifestation in the Church, then in the sacraments we can say we see and touch it. Edward Schillebeeckx and others have shown how the Church itself as a whole is Sacrament, a view affirmed by the Second Vatican Council. Everything about the Church is sacramental: the people, the ministry, the liturgy, the Scriptures, the pastoral care and selfless service, the music and the art, the church buildings and places of worship, the writings, the traditions of prayer, the religious communities, and so on, all bodying forth this mystery-filled belonging-together with God. All imperfect, all holy, windows onto the divine, not accidentally, but by explicit divine intention. It isn't possible to get close to the complete truth without getting close to the muck and looking for God in it. The incarnation did not content itself with choosing the nice bits—it is to be found through working on the unedifying bits too. It is in this kind of way that we can talk about the Church (and religious communities within it) as being holy.

Can you overdo it?

If in the churches of the Reformation there has been a tendency to undervalue the Church, in the Roman Catholic Church the problem takes a different form, reflecting a body in which law and its policing can often (but not always) loom large. In addition to the problems already mentioned, there is then the additional one of devaluing the Mystery by subjecting it to a humanly calibrated system. In this situation, the human, institutional Church is not circumscribed or put in its place, but the opposite—it is made all-wise, vetting everything by a kind of command-and-control system, and so paradoxically making the whole setup prosaic. Thankfully this is only one attitude in the Roman Catholic Church, and it no longer has free play. But the system was deeply formed by it, and it remains a problem, a brake on the Church's huge potential for carrying forward the gospel with imagination. In the end, such systematic reliance on the power of the institution is human-centredness in another form. An outsider like myself has a right to say this, because it affects all of us. We have to keep our eyes on the great and perplexing divine panorama, similar to but greater than the awesome revelations of the Hubble Telescope up above, while lurking too, to our even greater perplexity, within the mess on our own front drive.

The Church, then, is holy, a charged context in which Jesus has planted us. We cannot get close to him without coming into contact in some way with his creation, the Church. As we are looking at practices in the life of faith and prayer, there is a skill we need to learn, which comes with practice—in fact with practices: it is an innate sense that the Church is there. The nun or monk spends their life growing in the awareness that Jesus is there, Jesus is simply with us, among us, in the people around us, and this Jesus is not an isolated Palestinian bachelor—he is a family. The family of the Church is like a thronged force field where Jesus is in one sense the heart, and in another the whole Body. We have an open invitation, warmly extended, to join Christ in the great divine panorama, and this is a key to prayer.

My prayer is our prayer

What it means for prayer is this: I know that as a member of the Church I am never alone when I pray. I am praying with millions of others, on earth and in heaven. Whenever I am praying the Lord's Prayer, others the world over are praying it at the same time. Also, there are people in many places praying for me without my knowing. (Think for instance of all those petitions—"we pray for all health workers", "we pray for the people of Ukraine", "we pray for all families"). When I pray, I need a habit of reminding myself of this before I start. If I develop this habit, it will gradually become part of my mental furniture: it will become more and more how I live prayer. We have mentioned how, for a member of a family, the family is simply, tacitly there in the background all the time. This is the same thing. We can go further: prayer is God's work, not ours, it goes on all the time, and all we need to do is to step into it, like stepping onto an escalator. The Book of Revelation speaks of a great hymn rising from the whole of creation up to God. In the words of John Ellerton's hymn:

> We thank you that your Church, unsleeping
> while earth rolls onward into light,
> through all the world its watch is keeping,
> and never rests by day or night.

> As o'er each continent and island
> the dawn leads on another day,
> the voice of prayer is never silent,
> nor dies the strain of praise away.

The prayer of the Church goes on perpetually and we step into it; this is flying with the Holy Spirit, as we are brought to take part in the loving communion between the Father and the Son. My own prayer is God at work, and by grace it is me at work too. Never is it "the alone struggling to talk to the alone". Another hymn in illustration of this is Charles Wesley's "Let saints on earth in concert sing":

> For all the servants of our king
> in Earth and Heaven are one . . .
> One family, we dwell in him,
> one Church, above, beneath . . .

So whenever I pray, the first thing I do is recall the Church, which is Christ's Body. That is always the starting point. The Church is in the room, and we greet her. As this becomes a habit it becomes unconscious, part of our grain, innate.

Getting a more accurate picture of the Church

One thing that can hold us back from this is a frustrating fact: many people do not see the face of the Church. By this, I mean that clergy and members of religious communities on the whole can get a fair idea of what is going on in the worldwide Church. We know something about the different kinds of people working for the gospel, the kind of work they do, the problems they come up against. There is knowledge of the Church and the arts, the Church and politics, and so on. A lot of this tends only to be picked up by the "professionals": for the vast majority of Christians, do we really *know* the Church? Many do not, and get little help with knowing it. It is encouraging to know examples of dedicated and joyful Christian living and service in many parts of the world, or on our own doorstep; it can be a huge help simply to have caught their spirit, full of the resurrection. It deepens our knowledge to learn some Church history; it increases our responsibility if we are well aware of problems facing the Church in the contemporary world. Many Christians do not get much help in developing a small picture of the Church into a bigger one. If our prayer is to come alive, we need not only training in Christian practices, but training in knowledge of the Church as it really is. We need to see the Church's physical face—to see all that is going on which can be inspiring and energizing. Many Christians only see the equivalent of a chin or a nose, or perhaps pimples—there is a great deal more. An important part of this is face-to-face contact, for example visiting other churches, church projects or church groups; having some exchanges with other Christians; and, if we are lucky enough to go abroad, looking for ways to engage with the local church. But audiovisual means like YouTube can get you a long way in gaining this knowledge of the true face of the Church. Corporate self-knowledge should be a priority in Christian education.

Not just community, but communion

The picture of all Christians belonging in a universal community is a powerful one, but that hasn't yet said enough, and for a greater understanding we need to turn to the Greek word *koinonia*, which in English translations of the New Testament is often rendered by such words as "fellowship" or "participation". The English word that perhaps comes closest is "communion". The word "communion" conjures up a picture of human beings relating closely, like a loving couple, or a pair of old friends enjoying intimate conversation over a late-night glass of wine. The Christian notion of communion certainly includes something like this, but its true nature is a bit more demanding to grasp. If we think of an average human family, there may be moments of intense human relating, but most of the time, communion or *koinonia* in a family finds its more natural place at a different level: not like the two old friends sharing a glass of wine, or the lovers looking into each other's eyes, but more as something quietly sitting there in the background—there is a sense of unity deep down in our foundations, an innate awareness of the relationships being settled. Of course not all families are quite like that, and yet it is still possible, even in many of the worst cases, to talk in terms of a "communion" that is truly there, if not necessarily very exalted.

The early Christians went to great lengths to sustain a sense of communion. They were often incredibly bad at it, as we can see in some of St Paul's more bracing utterances, but we can see from the Epistles that they were close-knit groups, worshipping in one another's houses (probably the larger houses of better-off members), and there was a considerable emphasis on care for members in need. Once the Church had received its freedom under Constantine and began to grow in seriously large numbers, how was this to be sustained in large churches with huge congregations, without losing that sense of communion? What they did was to generate a large array of roles in the liturgy, sufficient to give a sense that these members of the group were representing everyone, so that all those present could sense that "this is ours". There were bishops, priests, deacons, servers, candle bearers, doorkeepers, singers, keepers of order, "parish" associations such as fledgling monastic groups. Early Syrian witnesses speak of virgins, both male and female, gathered round the altar, and so on. Roles and practices were also quickly developed in the liturgy to ensure the collecting of supplies for the needy, and for orphans and widows. Food banks are nothing new. Today we often fail to make sufficient use of roles in our worship, when it is one of the ways in which the worship manifests the people of God in all their variety, and encourages a sense of corporate communion. This has never been lost in monastic life, where roles in worship are as a matter of course shared out among the members.

One corollary of this is that people praying the Daily Prayers of the Church on their own can realize that not only are they not alone, but they are joining in with the whole Church, carried by it to some extent, and in addition they are fulfilling a role (we are back to Paul's image of the organs of the body). The housebound person, by joining in this worldwide network of action, is fulfilling a role in the liturgy, contributing a sense that "this is us", and God is with not just me, but us. The scenario that this assumes can perhaps help encourage parish communities to start doing their stuff in the Daily Prayer which is necessary for their flourishing.

Finding communion when it doesn't seem to be there

If the Church is communion, then it is difficult to talk about communion (*koinonia*) as one element among many, because it is everything. Either a Christian group is a *koinonia* or it is sub-Christian. The divine *koinonia* is fundamental to the Church's mission. It is the only thing of any serious worth that Christians have to give people. In many contemporary parishes and individual worshippers, this is a shadow of itself. How can awareness be awakened? I remember the day when I looked at the moon in daylight, where it seemed a blueish crescent in a blue sky. I noted where the sun was, and where its light fell on the moon, and made an effort to see the moon as a 3D sphere. All of a sudden, I saw it with a sense of shock. This sphere was suddenly very near—within the world I inhabit—a 3-dimensional object whose nearness could be felt. Every time I repeat the exercise I get the same shock, as sight of the moon in daylight suddenly flips into 3D—try it for yourself and see. Stories of conversion experiences are like this: the person suddenly sees for the first time. Gaining a sense of the divine gift of communion is like suddenly seeing in 3D. And as with my experience with the moon, certain moves need to be made in order to continue to see it. These moves are the common practices of the Christian *koinonia*.

Difficulties

Real communion is realistic. There are always difficulties where any group of people live together. We normally see them as problems to be avoided or planned around, but in the monastic tradition they are a key part of the journey to God. In any difficulty with another person, God is waiting for you. I am fond of quoting the story about St Bernard on a visit to a monastery where they said they had very good community life and got on well with each other. His response was to say that they had better start recruiting some difficult people, in order to grow in patience, charity, and self-knowledge. Every parish congregation needs a willingness to grow in patience with one another, charity towards one another, and self-knowledge. The best way to go with difficulties is neither away from them nor around them, but through them. One of the Desert Fathers said that the difficult brother is my physician. Too often there are difficulties between people in a firm, say, or in politics, or any group where people cooperate, problems which fail to come to any good resolution but drag on. Perhaps monastic texts about difficulties with other people ought to be read regularly in such groups—the *Sayings of the Desert Fathers*, for instance.[14] All these wise people are doing is distilling the basics of the New Testament: in Colossians for instance we read: "Clothe yourselves with compassion, kindness, humility, meekness, and patience. Bear with one another and, if anyone has a complaint against another, forgive each other" (Colossians 3:12–13). In a religious community it can be unbearable not to make your peace with your brother or sister before the sun goes down. But the parish too is called to be a communion, a place of reconciliation, and this ought to be, but often is not, an absolute gold standard. There is a point here that we must not miss, and it is that the difficulties are not problems getting in the way of communion, but elements in the discovery of it. Just as you cannot separate the failings of the Church from its majesty, its nature as Mystery, so in human community all the failings and difficulties are where God is waiting for us; they are not simply problems getting in the way.

Blessed in the Trinity

The next thing to add is that in religious communities the other members are in different ways often an inspiration and an example to each other. Over the years, you learn from the good you see in your sisters and brothers, and you pick up good things that have come from them but become part of you. Again, this will be true of any Christian group in good heart—they will know each other well enough to discover things that are attractive, that inspire and amuse. In the second century, the

---

14   See Benedicta Ward (ed.), *The Sayings of the Desert Fathers* (Kalamazoo, MI: Cistercian, 2004).

North African writer Tertullian spoke of this fact striking many outsiders: "'Look,' they say, 'how the Christians love one another.'"[15]

Notions about "community" that we find in the everyday of our secular society, except in some exceptional places, are too limited by comparison. There is a difference between straightforward human notions of community and the life of the gospel. In the Body of Christ, we are no longer talking simply in terms of how people relate together, but about the nature of God. God is perfect communion, the communion found between the Father, the Son and the Holy Spirit, in a circle of perfect love. Astonishingly, we are invited in. Christ (who is our sister and brother and mother and father) brings us into his eternal prayer to the Father, gathered together in the Holy Spirit. When we pray with the Church, in the *koinonia*, the "blest communion", we are going into that prayer of the Beloved. Every local Christian community is a communion: not, as we have seen, meaning soulful intensity with one another—that would sound laughable in many a church congregation—it is a communion because it is planted in the divine Communion. If a local congregation worships with a poor sense of the Church universal on earth and in heaven, or without a strong sense of living together in mutual love, it cannot fully access that communion or be it. It will be to some degree still human-centred.

In order to discover a whole-person way of praying, inward and personal on the one hand, and physical and bodily on the other, it can only be Christian if we see it not as a personal project, but as a joining into something bigger than ourselves, the communion of the Church. That will change the way we look at things, and change the way our Christian life is.

This brings us back to where we started. We assume faith to be a deeply personal thing, and this needs to be put in its proper place, not enthroned as the be-all and end-all. Of course faith is personal and needs to engage our deepest selves, but it is also participation with others in the communion of the Church, and this means that in many ways the Church holds our faith for us. When I pray, my faith goes up and down, but that's OK, because I am carried by the faith of the Church—all carrying each

---

[15] Tertullian, *Apologeticus* 39.7.

other, our boat held in its course by the wind of the Holy Spirit. It is always a mistake to think that in work, or family, or any enterprise with others, "I am indispensable." No one is indispensable—we depend on each other, and if one of us is taken out of the team either temporarily or permanently, through illness or some other accident of life, things will still go ahead in a different way. Neither am I indispensably in charge of my own prayer and life of faith. It doesn't depend just on me, but also on all those with whom I am bound together in the communion of the Body of Christ, all living stones in one holy Temple. So we should relax and allow ourselves to go with the flow.

Using our imagination

If you are a down-to-earth practical person, then what we have been saying may seem far-fetched. The idea of being united with so many people in prayer, and of prayer going on all the time as something there that we simply need to join in—aren't we just being asked to imagine all this? Just as you might say to someone who thinks they have seen a ghost: "You've just imagined it." Head-in-the-clouds people do certainly need to learn to be down-to-earth and practical for their own good and everybody else's, but the opposite is true as well. Modern psychology has shown that down-to-earth people need to discover their imaginations— not in the sense of imagining we have seen a ghost, but more as turning our attention to things that lie below the surface. We are using the word "imagination" here, then, not to mean concocting something unreal in our minds, but rather allowing ourselves to pick up real messages, feelings, intuitions, that lie nestling under the surface of our life. Jesus worked hard all the time to try and get people to use their imaginations; he was all the time refusing to give foursquare answers. His favourite way of helping things dawn on us (like seeing the moon in 3D) was to tell stories. His stories touch so many triggers that you can't reduce them simply to a list of "meanings". Think of the parable of the good Samaritan. There are clear messages that can be put in a list: loving our neighbour, having compassion, being generous, not dismissing strangers and people we look down on (both leading characters in the story fit those parts).

However, simply to trot out this list of things does not do what the story does; it fails lamentably to give us the power of the story or its full range of nudges. Imagination responds to hidden nudges in things, it takes us beyond simple information and facts, and ignites memories and images we might not have known were in us. If you look at a work of art, it can stir things up in you—you move on, and then another person comes along, and it stirs up slightly different things in them. The world of the imagination touches on the unpredictable hidden life of our nature.

In his disciples, Jesus was faced with a pretty down-to-earth lot, slow at responding to imaginative language. In Mark 8:13–21, they had all got into a boat to cross the lake: "Now the disciples had forgotten to bring any bread; and they had only one loaf with them in the boat. And he cautioned them, saying, 'Watch out—beware of the yeast of the Pharisees and the yeast of Herod.' They said to one another, 'It is because we have no bread.' And becoming aware of it, Jesus said to them, 'Why are you talking about having no bread? Do you still not perceive or understand?'" For Jesus, yeast is sinister stuff that can totally change a lump of dough through its mysterious working—a good image for the subtly corrupting people he was warning the disciples against. The disciples, meanwhile, had physical bread on the brain and couldn't get beyond it. In John's Gospel, Jesus frequently speaks of "signs"—things that are done or that happen, which speak to the imagination. In John 6:26, he says to the disciples who had come searching for him, "You are looking for me, not because you saw signs, but because you ate your fill of the loaves." In this story too, the disciples were interested in the bread, and had not reflected on the strange way it had got into their mouths. In all four Gospels, this group of fishermen are notoriously slow on the uptake—they are all the time being pushed to see things with the imagination and it doesn't come at all easily.

Too much imagination

Sometimes, however, the problem is the other way round: people can be too absorbed in their imagination to take seriously what is real—the practical needs around them. In Mark 7:9–13, the Pharisees and Scribes are so obsessed with the wonderful, inspiring Temple that they encourage people to give it money that ought to be used for maintaining their parents. This lovely, beautiful thing outshone for them people's boring practical needs (and moral responsibilities). The psychologist Carl Jung is credited as saying that our life's task is to work towards our opposite—in other words, if you are an artistic, imaginative, head-in-the-clouds person, you need to learn to take practical life seriously. Down-to-earth, practical people, on the other hand, need to discover the world of the imagination, of the deep things that can be stirred in us by stories, art, music, and stopping to think and reflect. The balanced Christian will be hands-on with all their practical responsibilities while also drawing life from the world of the imagination. But let's not be too individualistic: this can sound like a recipe for equalizing everybody. There is a corresponding truth that every community contains different gifts, and they contribute to each other and to a balanced and lively life in the community. In my community, we have brothers who are very head-in-the-clouds, brothers who are very practical, and everything else in between. The art is in turning all this into a Symphony. For every individual, on the other hand, a bit of imagination is needed for the Christian life, and also some basic down-to-earthness—that is where Jung's insight can be helpful for us, because Jesus is down-to-earth, but also stretches our imaginations.

When we come to pray, therefore, and start by uniting ourselves with the prayer of the universal Church, this uniting ourselves with the Church is no mere trotting out of doctrine or concocting of nice images—it asks of us an exercise of the imagination. Our transformed herd instinct is to become a kind of pride and reverence for the Church (which is, however, at the expense of nobody—it is a pride that is not competitive). It will touch the affections and will be supported by the Christian texts and art and music and liturgy that have a place in our lives, and the inspiring people who manifest the good cheer of the gospel, all of them showing us the face of Christ. To make a good Bolognese sauce for pasta, you need to simmer everything together for several hours, while the different ingredients gradually meld into a unified uniqueness. That is what can happen in the process of growing into praying with a sense of the Church, as all these ingredients gradually come together into a living awareness always there at the back of our minds. This awareness is not a feeling or a thing, but a person, Christ—we are seeing the face of Christ.

Alternation

After I left university, I got a job teaching in Italy. I was contacted while I was there by Brother Harold, mentioned in Chapter 3. He wanted to found a small centre for contemplative prayer—which later came to be called the Hermitage at Shepherds Law—would I be able to drive him around central Italy visiting hermitages to gain experience? We set off in my stuttering Wolseley 1500 for the depths of Umbria, and what came next was an extraordinary experience. We would arrive at a Franciscan hermitage in the depths of nowhere to be received hospitably by two or three brothers leading a hidden corporate life of prayer. On the way to the next hermitage, we would stop off at bed-and-breakfast in a town, then on to another hermitage, then another town, and so on. As we went around, we talked about the monastic tradition. The effect of this was an alternation between two worlds: the quiet presence of God in an ancient, hidden, holy place, then a modern town busy with tourists, shops and bustle, then again into the quiet atmosphere of prayer uninterrupted through the centuries. The experience left me with an unforgettable sense of God's presence, God's voice, in these miniature monasteries, and the interaction of that with the modern secular world, where God was present in a completely different way. That alternation acted like a magnifying glass on both the character of the modern world and the character of monastic places of prayer.

Later I would regularly lose this sense, and let the modern world provide the foundation for my common sense. God was in people and in the events of every day in ordinary life. That was what the gospel was about. Every now and again, I would visit a monastery, and each time be pulled back with a shock to things I had lost a feel for, to the God I was watering down, and to a sense of the Church. Then I would go off and it would soon melt away again. As a curate, I started full of enthusiasm for doing exciting things and trying to understand the gospel in the light of people's everyday lives: I thought the Church was stuffy and out of touch. My prayer life shrank to very little. Then one day I was standing in a front room talking with a man whose mother had just died, and realized he needed me to talk about God, and I felt a fraud. At that moment, all the teaching I had received at St Paul's Leicester and in college, and with Brother Harold, and in visits to monasteries, surfaced like a submarine: I had to get back to praying seriously, and had to work at bringing together in myself the worlds of parish, modern world and monastery.

Climate

Monasteries and convents, in fact all houses of religious brothers and sisters, hold in common a particular characteristic: they are microclimates. You go into them and feel the difference. This climate is not simply generated by the members of the community, and it is not something automatic. Nuns and monks are imperfect people who are setting apart a particular place and living in it a particular life, and this life simply does things to these people and to the place they are living it in. What it does is not an effect, although it does have effects. It is not a thing but Christ's presence. This life holds before the Church what the Church is called to be. It is a kind of prophecy, a sign, a place that holds the line. It is like the pilot light in a gas appliance—burning all the time. People of the Middle Ages fell into the trap of concluding from this that nuns and monks lived the perfect life, while ordinary people had to make do with something less. Thankfully we have moved away from that and returned to older sources. Monastic life is an organ in the body. It has a particular function in the Body of Christ, working in conjunction with all the other organs. Somebody has to do it, and somebody also has to do all the other things, in an equal playing field. Other Christians have a much more difficult and heroic task as their challenge—how to live the gospel in a world that shouts it down all the time. For them it is easy to grow weary and give up the fight. By comparison monks and nuns may be having it easier.

We come back to what has been said about the Church. If we are going to pray with a sense of praying with the whole Church, and being encouraged and sustained by that, we need a microclimate to which we can regularly return. Every parish, every Christian group, needs to see how it can be a microclimate. We can see the microclimate developing already in the gospel. Jesus, when he began his ministry, immediately gathered around him a small group that he worked with to build up a new way of seeing things fired by the imagination. The group would go apart, it had its own life, and this was a strength to Jesus' ministry and theirs. This is not about escaping into a fantasy world, a churchy corner where we can escape from the demands of life. It is life in Christ. There is always a chemistry between the gospel and the world around us. If we only become steeped in the world around us, there will be no chemistry, no shocks to anybody's system. The microclimate of the Church is there to exist in chemistry with everyday life, and is about nothing less than what is *real*, the reality of God, who is known in the world around us, on the bus and in the workplace, but also—and this is vital—in going apart to communicate with God in specific ways and places that are not easily found in that world, such as monasteries, churches, places of prayer; in other words, groups that live in a way that is different from the life all around them.

My faith is our faith

If you struggle with the ability to believe, and if you cannot get yourself to pray, or to do it as well as you would like, the first thing to recognize is that you cannot do it on your own in this isolated, personal way. You need to find a way of climbing aboard the Church and gaining a sense that you are not alone, and that the People of God have resources to share. This "climbing aboard the Church" may not be so much about believing, as about taking steps, doing something: learning about the contemporary Church and its life, getting engaged with other people in it, and doing the things it does. Belief comes out of experience, not out of scratching our heads. I and you are wired up, not to be isolated individuals, but to be persons-in-community.

We all need community, if not all in the same way or at the same level. The best and most well-grounded form of community will be found in what Jesus brought, in taking our primordial herd instincts, our capacity for team spirit, our hard-wiring for community, and encouraging us into something new that transforms these instincts into their truest manifestation: the divine society of the Church, the model of all community, and the source of all the life that true communities need. What religious communities are seeking to live is simply this: to be the Church in this place.

Summary

Where are we so far? The exploration started with religious orders and their life, noting the life was filled with practices. This led to an unexpected recognition: that in religions, people normally start by practising, and only then does belief begin to grow, like the trust that grows gradually in a new friendship. You don't need to "believe" everything before you start trying to live as a Christian, you start by attempting it and you just see. We then looked more closely at the question of practices and recognized that they need to be set in a particular context, that of having a "sense of the Church". The Church is a mixed bag of human beings behaving well and behaving badly, and we have to take that as a central part of the chemistry that is going on, recognizing all the time that the Church is bigger than any of that—it is divine, holy, the Body of Christ—a mystery. Its "practices" look different when seen like this.

If gaining a sense of the Church is a "skill" that grows in us through participation in its doings, there is a second "skill" for us to grow in if we are to get very far. We have painted what might be called a two-dimensional picture of the Church, and we now need to look at it in the round.

5

It's genetic

Now it is time to look at something that is essential, the practice of following Jesus, and I'll start with a sort of parable. If the reader has patience with me, the message will eventually become clear. Here, to start with, is a riddle such as Samson might have set (see Judges 14:12–18).

What is it that is:

Essential, but often overrated;
unable to exist without us, but also has a life of its own;
always changing, but remains what it is;
trustworthy, but often misleading;
created by us, but we could never sit down to create it;
has tight rules, but with it we can soar above our limitations.

The answer is: language. Language is all those partly contradictory things and a lot more. If we explore the characteristics of language, we find they illustrate something about the gospel, and even the simple business of being human beings.

Language is essential for cooperation between humans and for people to form into groups and nations. It is ancient, going back thousands of years: in order to understand it, we often have to burrow through millennia, as we clarify meanings of words by finding their etymology. For instance, the word "company" derives from the Latin *cum* (with) and *pane* (bread). From that, we see the importance of eating together as a source of human cooperation and sociability.

Our particular language shapes the way we think—many of my thoughts are what they are because they have been shaped by the English language. For this and other reasons translation is never without problems. Say, for instance, you live in Italy and someone insists something must be done. They are wanting to be firm with you, because you ought in their opinion to be doing this thing well, and in due time. They are worried that you won't. And so they say, "*Mi raccomando, eh?*" This appears to be saying, "I recommend myself, eh?" to puzzled English listeners—they could not know that it really means something like "I insist on this", but as a translation that is too strong. There is no equivalent in English. What would an English speaker say in this situation, if they wanted to be sure you are going to do a thing properly and in due time? "Is that clear?" perhaps, but that is more threatening than the Italian phrase. In fact, there is no adequate equivalent in English. We would have to do it by the face we pulled, or some kind of roundabout words. Then I am standing at an Italian supermarket checkout. An old lady has been talking about her ailments, and as she goes, the woman at the till says, "*Mi raccomando, eh?*" I scratch my head. This time it means something like "look after yourself".

It is a strange fact that often the way we say things in our particular language shapes the way we think. I can think a particular thing about a situation, while people speaking another language will have their thoughts about the same situation shaped in a different way. The German art historian E. H. Gombrich spent most of his adult life as a British citizen. He says he finds, when showing a group of Germans around the National Gallery and talking in German, he says slightly different things about the artworks than when talking to British groups. The way phrases are composed in a language can be peculiar to that language, and turn our thoughts about things into particular shapes that can't be transferred into another language. In English, we might think of the word "worship", a powerful and resonant word for which there is no equivalent in other cultures. In Latin languages, for instance, you have to speak of "adoration" or "cult". Language is fundamentally important to us, and it is important to try and understand what is going on in it.

In ways akin to this, Christianity is a "language", and this is not something to be treated at all lightly. It is an old and deep language, and just as in a normal language we look up the origins of words to help us understand, so also in Christianity we have to search the past in order to understand the present properly. It also sets us to think in particular ways, which can be a bit different from how people think who are outside the Christian "language". We do many things in church without knowing why we do them, and their history can throw light on them. For instance, how many people know that when Jesus "gave thanks" at the Last Supper, what he will have said (or, more likely, half-sung, something like a Martin Luther-King sermon) would have been a clear ancestor of the Eucharistic Prayers in contemporary Roman Catholic, Orthodox, Anglican, Methodist, Lutheran and other services? And even more surprising, these prayers in all the churches are very similar to a prayer used in the synagogue today by Jews. That affects how we look at this long prayer—it goes back to Jesus. And if we look at the history of it between then and now, we learn a lot more, leading us to see it with different eyes. Similar things can be said about much of Christian worship, and not only that but also theology, doctrine and pastoral practice. The Bible is not an off-the-shelf manual for setting up a way of living, as if the gospel were flat-pack furniture; the Bible is itself a part of the "language" of Christianity.

The "language" of the Church

We have in the Church inherited all sorts of practices that could have been different in many ways, and the form they take now may not be absolutely necessary. They could have been otherwise, but they are what we have received, and all together they add up to a language like English.

Can the life of religious communities throw light on this for us? In the opening chapters, I mentioned a range of practices typical of monastic life. Many of them are quite strange and counter-intuitive: for instance, the renunciation of personal property. This seems an odd thing to embrace, and particularly alien in a society where so much is available easily and can be beneficial. We can begin to understand this item in the "language" of monastic life by tracing its origins. This takes us back to the primitive Church—in Acts 2:45, "they would sell their possessions and goods and distribute the proceeds to all, as any had need". If you are to live community radically, then nothing must be there to get in the way. More insight into this monastic practice can come from other parts of the New Testament, and as you trace it through the centuries you find a deepening wisdom about it. Religious communities have, for instance, wrestled with the fact that the practices described in Acts 2 and 4 are self-defeating without some adjustment. Literally to sell all your possessions and give the proceeds to the poor would leave you with no way of staying alive. Ways needed to be found of making it workable in the world in which the community is set. The Benedictine tradition, for instance, practices "community of goods"—no one owns anything, but the community as a whole has whatever it needs in order to live its life as portrayed in the Rule of St Benedict. At the same time St Benedict was fierce about individuals having no possessions (see Rule of St Benedict Chapter 33). The way this has worked has continually changed as society has changed. For instance, in my own community, brethren are not allowed to dispose of any capital they come with. They retain legal ownership of it but cannot exercise that ownership or benefit from it. This is partly a matter of justice to other family members who may have proper call upon it, and partly for reasons of current British law.

Religious communities, however, are only living in a concentrated form what is the calling of all Christians. Christ's call to all of us to turn from self carries with it unavoidable consequences for self-renunciation, sharing what we have, and living in the realization that we can take nothing with us when we die. The monastic limiting or renunciation of personal property simply seeks to follow to the hilt a truth of the gospel that is for everybody, firmly rooted as it is in the life of the primitive Church and the precepts of the gospel. We dig down into the Christian "language" through the centuries in the quest to understand a thing like this.

The "language" of Christian practices is there to be taken seriously: the liturgy, the history of study of the Bible, the spiritual tradition, the theology and teaching, the ways we love and serve others, all the while making our own contribution to continual change and development. To take Christian practices seriously means to enable them to become second nature. In learning a language, the aim is to arrive at a point where we speak it with unselfconscious verve—we don't have to think about it, it just comes out. Going back to what we said in Chapter 3, our brain does not usually play a large part in the way we speak—it is our jaw and our tongue that know what to do. The same applies to the whole range of Christian practices—like waving to a friend across the road, you just do it.

Tradition

Each spoken language, such as English or French, is in fact a "tradition", all the time growing and developing like a plant, while going down to deep roots. This is what the Church is. The word "tradition" is often misused and misunderstood. It can be seen as something old and stuck, and some of us might in fact have an affection for things old and stuck: the changing of the guard, or half-timbered cottages (although even they get modern plumbing as they go along), or old ways of doing things we don't want to change. That is a superficial understanding of tradition. The primary meaning is more: like a living language, the Christian tradition has a long history behind it, but is full of life and constantly developing and changing, now and onwards into the future. It is like a plant: it never stands still—if a plant stops growing, it is dead. Anyone who has attempted to read Geoffrey Chaucer will have seen that language is always changing, and in our own time this proceeds at a pace, with coining of multitudes of new words and repurposing of old ones ("queer", for instance), not to mention the marching Americanization of British English. At the same time, local varieties flourish, and British local accents seem to be as vigorous as ever. This is the living tradition of the English language. A true tradition is always changing as it goes along. The composer Gustav Mahler said that tradition is tending the flame, not worshipping the ashes. Christianity sells itself short when it fails to understand this. The tradition is an incomparable driving force in various ways—a bearer of information we need, that could be called genetic, and a well from which to draw wisdom for our time. It is also nuts and bolts: the celebration of the Eucharist faithful to its trajectory through time; the Daily Prayer of the Church; the baptizing of new followers; the sacrificial love and service of others, from the deacons gathering supplies for the poor in the early Christian Eucharist to modern parish foodbanks.

The Christian language or tradition is no mere abstract concept—it is a practical reality of Christian flourishing.

Is tradition for today?

People rightly ask searching questions: does tradition as understood in this sense actually speak today? Is Christian tradition a living or a dead language? Among many Christians, the Tradition now is hardly allowed to speak. In the churches, there is widespread respect for the Tradition in various ways, great and small, but regularly it is merely treated as a "resource". The terrible and widespread use of the word "resource" in reference to those demanding gifts of worship, prayer, retreats, church buildings, and sacraments, says it all. It lays bare our assumptions that we are the masters: we identify our needs using our mere human abilities, and God provides things like tradition for us to plunder to help us meet those needs in ways we have determined for ourselves. We love some aspects of the Christian tradition, but as tools or props—"resources". What we have lost is an attention that is serious and sustained, where the Tradition becomes part of our mental furniture, part of how we tick. I have already been saying this about the Church, and we now add what goes with it: the Tradition, the Christian "language". One of the "skills" that Christ seeks to train us in, in a repeated exercise of the imagination, is to know instinctively that we are in the Church, and within its Tradition, its "language". In this we may need to give our brains a bit of a rest, and let our bodies and our whole being just live these things. We will never get there, however, if we continue to see them as things or ideas—they are about being in Christ. I often pray in front of an icon of Christ. A lot of the time I keep my eyes shut, but when I look I see him looking at me and feel the shock of Christ's sovereign, searching presence: I am put on my mettle, and in the very grain of these perceptions of mine are the Church and the Tradition.

The community as an orchestra

It may help to think of the Church and its tradition as an orchestra. Deep speaks to deep as the orchestra peer at their music and musicianship moves into action, becoming expansive beyond the printed notes as the music lifts off the page. The orchestra live and breathe the repertoire, so that years of playing Schubert affect how they play Stravinsky, and dips into jazz seem perhaps to come out in Beethoven, and Beethoven in the jazz. And what is this music? Mere sounds. It represents nothing, relates to nothing in our everyday world—it is an enclosed language, and yet universal. What does it do to us? How can you describe it? Certainly music can affect moods, it can evoke some sort of drama, but what on earth is it that can have such profound effects on us that go much further than mere mood? And it doesn't work unless you take your eyes off yourself and fly. By this, I mean that another orchestra could blink determinedly at the pages and plonk out note for note, and seats at concerts would be empty. Another way people can kill music is to have aims: to make people happy, or to have a rousing experience, say. True music is free, simply itself, taking us to things we could not imagine or plan, or perhaps even know we wanted. Music is like the sea, or the cosmos. It is just there.

Developing the repertoire

Monastic life is the life of an orchestra—it can't work unless the community embraces and sits under the repertoire, the Tradition. It will always fall short, but the fundamental framework never changes: the taming and conversion of the self, the channelling of desires, the bringing of all together in one fellowship of charity, the divine presence in the midst, through practices passed on by the Tradition. In answer to the question, "Is this monastic tradition a living or dead language—has it now come up against the buffers?", we face perhaps the toughest part of carrying any tradition forward today: what must our contribution be to enable this language to go forward and to change, as it must? For religious communities today, it is a real concern: what tough questions does the community need to ask about what needs to change in its life, considering how contemporary society is now so different from all that has been before? How can the community best use the internet and social media? How far is it sensible to make use of credit cards or smartphones?

The contrast between the life of religious communities and that of everyone else has never been so stark. If a young person explores whether to move from life in modern society to join a religious community, the renunciations and changes required will be much bigger than a hundred years ago. In the streets around my own community, people in those times knew what obedience was, and chastity, and community, and stability—but no longer, much. We have to ask how far this has a bearing on the fall in recruitment to religious communities. Since the 1960s, vocations have fallen dramatically. In British Anglican communities, the fall is as great as in the Roman Catholic Church. It is natural to ask whether we cannot make some changes to meet people halfway, for instance by enabling the kind of temporary membership practised in Buddhism. There is one Anglican community, the Melanesian Brotherhood in Papua New Guinea, that does exactly this, very successfully, but it is difficult to translate to Europe from that very particular culture.

There is already scope within many communities for people to join temporarily—for instance, in my own community the final decision on whether to make a permanent commitment can, in some cases, wait up to nine years. It can take time and careful communication to overcome misunderstandings—misunderstandings not only about religious community life, but also about life in our contemporary society.

One particular misunderstanding that requires time to unpack is our concept of freedom. The possibility of surrendering many of the freedoms we enjoy in modern life looks really daunting. Freedom, however, is a weasel word. We think we know what it means, but if we examine it, we find it means something else. We think we have liberty of choice in our society and liberty of movement, whereas we are determined by a whole host of factors. How many married people can go where they want when they want? How many people in the workplace can escape the requirements of obedience? Compared with a hundred years ago, many of our freedoms have in fact been dramatically diminished: we are now like Gulliver, tied down by a thousand threads of Health and Safety, good practice regulations, employment law, and so on, all of them producing benefits, but at the same time limiting previous freedoms. You cannot seem to move in any direction without coming up against regulations. I know this myself from teaching in a university just as new controls were coming in. Many pieces of good practice were introduced, which increased communication, fairness, better care for students, and so on. But at the same time the teacher and class felt less and less free to fly, and more and more as if you were plonking out gobbets of information to satisfy determined "outcomes". I exaggerate, but what exactly do we mean when we say we value our freedoms? In the parish, the same issues apply. Parish priests are more constrained and less free today, and many in our congregations wrestle with the tension between all the demands (and constraints) of modern life, our desire for "freedom", and the invitation from Christ to commit ourselves to the gospel in ways that will cost something. Just as in monastic life, the problem of being committed Christians has a lot to do with our aspiration to "freedom". A superficial perception of "Tradition" can conjure up a picture of being confined to tramlines. Between tramlines and liberty, however, there is a way that is greater than both, and this can be illustrated from the arts.

True freedom

We all flourish through challenges. Michelangelo is once supposed to have looked at a very unpromising piece of rock and said, "Constraint is life, freedom is death." The challenge to respond to the difficulties presented by the rock pushed him into yet another triumphant breakthrough of the imagination. Without that awkward piece of rock, he would never, given complete freedom, have imagined what he in fact produced. In the New Testament, the glorious liberty of the children of God (Romans 8:21) is a free gift that comes through the Holy Spirit, who is with us in our struggle. It is not an end in itself, as "freedom" can be in the imagined ideals of modern society. The end is God, the journey is struggle, and freedom is discovered in the midst of all this as a kind of miracle, one of the gifts of being with God. The "language", the Tradition, of the Church is, it could be said, a form of fruitful constraint, like Michelangelo's rock.

It can mistakenly be perceived as tramlines, but living tradition is more like a train travelling forward, laying its own tracks before it as it goes, in response to the terrain.

In monastic life, one measure of your calling is how free you seem to become. Not free to choose or buy this or that, not free to freewheel, not free to have no commitments or constraints, but free because of the gradual growing of, dare we use Paul's words, a "glorious liberty"; and yet again we find ourselves saying this is true of all Christian vocation and applies to everybody. The Church is an orchestra whose music-making enables it to fly in ways it could never have dreamed of, as a kestrel must exult in the tense but energizing constraint of its hovering in the free air.

Our picture of what it is to be a human being

The challenges to living in a tradition today are pretty huge, and destined to grow. Changes in our understanding of what it is to be human beings are beginning to move apace—where will the developments on gender lead us? Where will the dominant individualism lead us? Where will science lead us? Artificial intelligence is now beginning to outshine what human brains can do. You can spend time looking at the achievements of modern electronics and have the weird sensation, when turning to regard the human body, that it begins to look dated. There is now talk of adapted bodies, adapted brains, and cyborgs, where human beings become a harnessing-together of human bodies (or what will be left of them) with electronic devices. These things will start to happen, and not under the guidance of the wisest minds (to judge from some of the people who write about them). The opportunities but also the dangers are great, because our society is not in a good position to appreciate adequately what it means to be a human being.

How is the monastic tradition to respond to these moves away from humanity as we have known it, and from traditional understandings of what a human being is? How are all Christians to respond? All we can say is that responding is going to be tough. The carrying-forward and developing of the living tradition, as it ever changes, has never been so much of a head-scratcher as it is proving to be today. It has never been easy, and wrong paths can be taken; but the right way forward can never be found if we do not first embrace the tradition as we have received it. Then we need to be sure we are listening for the voice of Christ in our times—in our society, and all its life and work and art and literature and sheer existential experience of life. From that, we have the task of matching the voice of Christ in the Church and its "language" with the voice of Christ in society.

The voice of Christ in our society

How is the voice of Christ present in our society? Among the parables of Jesus, the Good Samaritan is again a helpful example. The Samaritan was an outsider, not of the "true faith". Yet he is precisely the one who shows qualities of the gospel Jesus came to proclaim. As we look around us at our society, we can see plenty of love and respect for one another in all kinds of ways. Where love is, there is God. Even in an imaginary land where all may be atheists, wherever people love one another, even there the gospel is being lived; even there is the hidden, unrecognized presence of Christ. Sometimes secular society can see better than the Church, and recent scandals over abuse of minors is a sad example: the Church has been called to account by many people who claim no Christian faith. This being so, we come back yet again to what has been said before: just as in monastic life, it is the life itself which is to be held up as an example, and not necessarily the people who are living it, since they are all sinners. The Body of Christ is always something we can revere and have love for, while being realistic about its present human members: they do not always come off better in comparison with secular folk, and they may not always see implications of the gospel so well as people outside. This is one reason we have to attend to the Christ who is present and active in our society.

There is a second way that the gospel is incomplete without pairing up with ordinary practical human life. The gospel does not explain the practicalities of running a shop, even though it shows us principles for doing that well. It does not tell us how to bring up children or to cook. What the gospel does is pair up with human wisdom and experience.

Religious communities, for instance, nowadays take advantage of modern skills to do with being human beings together. They can make good, profitable use of psychiatrists, or of human sciences that work on how people live together in groups. Parishes similarly can benefit from safeguarding training; clergy can gain from studying teaching skills. In all of these, insofar as they are good, these "secular" things are God at work.

The problem lies in discerning. When do we have something to learn from society, when something to teach it, when must we stand against it? In what ways does monastic life need to change, and in what ways does it need to stand faithful to its treasure? One of St Benedict's famous pieces of advice is, "Always consult, and you will never regret your decisions."[16] Endless consultation, judicious testing of the waters, and patience are needed all the time. There is frequent discussion among religious sisters and brothers on such matters as how we use the internet, or whether and how we should reduce the great degree of contrast between ordinary life and that of religious communities. It is of the nature of religious communities that reflection should be well-informed and given plenty of time to "stew", like a good Bolognese sauce. One thing they never aim to do is to take life by the scruff of the neck. Taking time and being patient are part of the "language". Above all there is a quest for an overriding "sense" or consensus on where we should be going—you simply wait for that to emerge, and there are many contemporary questions on which that has not emerged yet in the monastic world. Perhaps we need to stay more or less as we are, but who can tell whether or not we are missing the boat in not making changes that future generations will see we should have identified?

Discerning the way forward in the wider Church

Just the same questions in their own way apply to the parish. How are we to adapt the Tradition that we have received in the right way for people today? There is a danger of misplaced judgements and wrong directions. Attempts to make worship attractive to people are often

---

[16]   Rule of St Benedict, 3.13.

based on poor understanding of the principles of worship and a lack of mature grounding in the things of God. In our relationship with the world around us, we have a vocation: to attend carefully to it, and to see how we may train our antennae. The vocation that comes to us from the gospel, however, is not to be lame followers, but to give a lead where a lead is needed. We must not be afraid to give a lead. At the moment, it is easy to fall into indiscriminate following of our society and culture. The other danger is to get everything principled and "right", but way above people's heads (it could be said that that happened with the Book of Common Prayer in the sixteenth century, which, with all its head-stuff, left the common people behind). Lord Reith put it well in talking of the BBC: "The BBC must lead, not follow, its listeners, but it must not lead at so great a distance as to shake off pursuit."[17] We need to pay the greatest attention to God-in-our-faith and to God-in-the-world. The aim of such attention would be not to work in a vacuum, but to carry forward and develop the Christian Tradition itself. The Tradition gives us a sense of being in a trajectory, rather than at a static point or no-man's-land. It gives a feel for the layeredness of the faith, a genetic sense, a sense of our position in time. It then goes further, beyond the limits of our senses: the Tradition is like the sea—who can measure it? Who can capture the effect it can have? It also lays a sense of responsibility on us to carry it forward so that it can remain in fruitful communication with the world around it. This raises another question: how can we live within the tradition and yet at the same time pursue free enquiry, rational evaluation, and a scientific approach to the Scriptures and the claims of faith? The Christian Tradition tells us that reason has its essential part to play.

---

[17]   *The Economist*, 29 January 2022, p. 71.

Monastic theology

There is something in monastic life that can help us here: the French monk and writer Jean Leclercq called it "monastic theology".[18] In a university, theology is pursued rationally and scientifically: religious beliefs are analysed according to scientific principles. This goes back to a revolution in theological study in the twelfth century which led to what has come to be known as scholasticism: this basically involves a reasoned, "scientific" examination of all the elements of Christian life and practice. Monasteries, however, stayed with an older way that was more holistic. To the tools of reason were added the life of prayer, life in community, and the gamut of monastic life. In other words, while in the universities the faith and God were put on a slab and dissected, in the monasteries the faith was inhabited by the whole person, with inquiry always being conducted in the context of prayer.

A partial parallel can be found in an experience of my own. At the time, I was teaching about the Christian liturgy in a secular university, I also taught the same subject in my community's theological college. I was made aware, in a weekly alternation, of the difference between teaching about worship in the one place and the other. In the university, I was to teach it "scientifically", with a disparate and interested university group (it included people of many religious backgrounds, non-believers, and sometimes Muslims), while in our college I was teaching it with students who were living and praying the liturgy corporately every day. With the one group it was inevitably dealt mostly with facts and information (left-side-of-the-brain stuff), and it was difficult to enable the students to discover the hinterland, while with our own students it was still scientific, but also "sapiential" (*sapientia* is Latin for "wisdom"), engaging more fully the right side of the brain and its capacity to embrace the whole experience, coordinating the information with the actual living of it— comprehending things with the whole of ourselves. Monastic theology is not concerned simply with items that you believe, but with a voyage arising from the life of prayer and worship in Christian community.

---

[18] Jean Leclercq, *The Love of Learning and the Desire for God* (New York: Fordham University Press, 1974).

You could say that key characteristics of "monastic theology" are a quiet patience that bides its time, an openness to everything, humility that avoids taking stances over against others, and the centrality of prayer. Pure science and cut-and-thrust have their place, but that place needs to be on the steps of the ladder, and not on the throne. "Monastic theology" is holistic, as the monastic life is holistic, lived with mind and body, things, places, practices and prayer, all within a climate that is alive.

The two approaches overlap, and each needs the other. However, it is important to be aware of the distinction. The relevance of this for the parish today can be seen if we think of people's attitudes to the resurrection of Christ. For many churchgoing Christians it is treated relatively unthinkingly as part of the package. If you sat down to try and think it out, you wouldn't know what to make of it, but you accept that it is part of the wallpaper and shrug your shoulders over any of the difficulties. By contrast, it seems from the New Testament that early Christians were energized by the resurrection—it was the heart of their faith and the source of their energy. We can see something of this in Eastern Orthodox Christianity, which makes such a wonderful festival of Easter. In the West, Easter slightly lost its shine at some point, so that what we have inherited is a bit less than the Eastern Orthodox experience.

If we are to help one another make this energizing connection with the resurrection of Christ, there are two possible approaches. One is to try and think it out by looking at the information and weighing the pros and cons. We can gain a lot of helpful insights that way, and there is an abundance of material to help us understand better the texts and their implications, and the various facets of the question. However, this approach can't give us the full picture because it principally takes the form of assembled information, like our list of elements in the story of the Good Samaritan. The stories of the resurrection and the references to it throughout the New Testament take us further, because they can engage our imagination, our feelings, our gut responses. Then we add to those New Testament stories the presence of the resurrection in the subsequent Tradition, particularly in the liturgy. We are then beginning to swim our way to the resurrection rather than think our way there. We swim in the Tradition and the liturgy, and we also start looking around us, especially at all those inspiring people who, because of the resurrection, display a joyful energy and faith that is something all of its own. In this way, in the Church's lived life, we meet the thing itself. For myself, one of the most telling places is the Paschal Vigil at Easter. I could almost say that I believe in the resurrection because of the Paschal Vigil. In it, we get swept up into the energy and life of Christ risen from the dead. Then if we go from there to read the accounts in the Scriptures, the stories begin to release their full secret, not by being dissected on a slab, but by being swum in.

Think of a group of actors: they are having a discussion about putting on a play about a celebrity. There is a twist: the actors are members of the celebrity's family. At a certain point, they call in the help of an academic who has researched the life of the celebrity and is expertly informed. The academic fills a lot of gaps in their knowledge—the family might exclaim, "Blimey—we didn't know that!" The academic also brings a fascinating view from the outside, correcting to some extent how this family sees the person and his life in the family. The academic, however, would not put on such a good play as these people can. She has the facts, they have the knowing: they know the person better than any complete stranger can, however much they study. But now comes another twist: they realize at a certain point they aren't going to put a play on after all—it could only be a travesty. It would fail to convey the "knowing" that is theirs alone.

The intimate life of that family is like monastic theology, like life in the Tradition. The risen Christ makes himself known to us when we participate in the Church family as true, full-blooded members. We won't be likely to stir people's hearts with mere facts about the resurrection, and neither are we likely to move them by staging things we have devised. We must make use of the reasoning faculties given to us by God, and pursue that to the hilt, but only participation in the actual family can in the end get us there.

Summary

The practices of Christianity are part of a great "language", which we call the Christian Tradition. We are all looking for freedom, and might be surprised to learn that it is tradition that can make us free. A true, living tradition does not limit life but expands it; it is always in dialogue with the society around it, for it is always faced with the question of how it should develop. Like football, it can only develop in the playing, not in simply sitting in a room to think about it, even if that might help. Our apprehension of truth and belief can only develop as we actually practise the practices of Christianity.

6

Practices

It is time now to look at Christian practices. I have been trying to show that, like any practices of any sort, they have the power to affect my memory and my inner self. Take a small animal, for instance: it eyes you suspiciously, trembling all over. You throw it a piece of grain—it eats it cautiously. After a few days of this it begins to pester you for grain—it has grown in trust through this physical practice. You and it have a lot in common. You both live with your whole being, both your body and your inner life. Faith is fostered through our body, and through doing things. Faith is also fostered through personal, interior enquiry, personal prayer, and the use of our reason. My body and my personal life are one thing, not two departments. They are just LIVED. I have said that we have grown up in a culture that has overemphasized the inner, the "personal", and underrated the body, sending it to the bottom of the ladder or even forgetting it is there altogether. Relating to Christ then becomes a rump of goings-on in the individual's head. If our soul needs to blend with our body to be one living thing, it is time now to explore what practices have the power to bring body and mind together. Not any old practices will do—Christian practices have this characteristic: they are stamped by their setting in the Church and the Christian Tradition. In exploring them, we start with the trunk of the tree and then work out along the branches.

Baptism

The tree's trunk starts with Baptism, as a person is plunged (if possible) in water in the name of the Trinity. This practice of Baptism sends reverberations through our lives, and awareness of this is nowadays being rediscovered. Our Baptism is the start-point and waymarker for the whole of our succeeding life. We have died with Christ and been reborn as members of Christ's Body. Once we were no people; now we are God's people. In monastic life, there is a link here that is part of our modern rediscovery of Baptism. In the early centuries, baptisms could be carried out in the same service as monastic professions. For the nun or monk, our life is simply a living-out of the consequences of our Baptism. Baptism is a re-making, the launch onto a life of conversion, and that is also what the monastic profession is. In the church of my community, we have a large total-immersion font where adults can be baptized by being plunged under water. Such fonts have in recent decades become increasingly common in parish churches, especially in America. You can see a good example in the Roman Catholic Church of St Charles Borromeo, Ogle Street, in London. Ours at Mirfield is a central focus at the west end of the church; at Eastertide the Sunday Eucharist begins at the font, and when a brother makes his life vows, this also begins there. Such returning to the font is for all of us. At Easter in the Paschal Vigil, for instance, the liturgy invites all Christians to return to the waters and renew their baptismal vows. When one of our brothers dies, in the procession out of the church we scoop up a bowl of water from the font and at the grave everyone takes a turn to sprinkle his coffin, using a sprig of rosemary. Baptism and death and life weave their way together.

An old tradition is for a small dish of baptismal water to stand by the church door so that we can dip our finger and touch our foreheads with the water to re-live our Baptism, in a return to the energy it gives, to the person of Christ. Other imaginative ways are being explored today to include the font in our worship. Baptism is the first Christian practice that any Christian gets involved in, and its echoes roll down through the rest of our life.

Eucharist

This leads us to the Eucharist. Among the many actions which the Gospels and Epistles pass on to us—touching, anointing, kiss of peace, baptizing with water, gathering, singing, signing ourselves with the cross of Calvary, renunciations, tongues, commissionings, and so on, we have this action which Jesus bade us do in a re-living of him. The English word "remembrance" is too weak: the Greek word used in the Gospels (*anamnesis*) means more. Our word "remember" means thinking about things that are dead and gone. The word Jesus used means to recall in such a way that it is all truly re-lived. Jesus' incarnation, ministry, death, resurrection and ascension are not dead and gone. They are real forever and the "in remembrance of me" plunges us in them as Baptism plunges us in them.

Jesus' instruction was to "do this". Very bodily, very corporate, an action to be done. On what is to be done the information is pretty clear: gathering at a table, taking bread and wine, giving thanks over them, breaking the bread, and distributing them, saying they are Christ's body and blood. With the "giving thanks over them", the New Testament gives no information on the words Jesus used in giving thanks, but this information has come to us from another source: it has been passed on to us in the Church's practice, down the centuries, with surprising consistency. Suffice here to say that this thanksgiving is for our redemption, and although it varies greatly, it follows a specific, traditional shape that can be found also in synagogue worship today. When Jesus had made his thanksgiving, he gave the bread and the wine to the disciples with the surprising words "this is my body" and "this is my blood". As we all know, there has been endless argument and disagreement on what he meant by this, but it is difficult to fault the view of Queen Elizabeth I: "'Twas God the word that spake it, He took the Bread and brake it, And what that word did make it, That I believe, and take it." Jesus was well aware that the world is full of people with an uncomplicated religious faith, and uncomplicated use of language, and if he didn't recognize his words would be taken at face value, he was more out of touch with real life than we know him to be. Whatever our views when it comes to teasing it out further, what is perfectly clear is that in this Eucharistic meal Jesus left people a practice to do. But such prosaic words hardly begin to do justice to the great exercise of the imagination he was wanting to lead us into—"this is my body, my blood" and then that most intimate of things—we eat and we drink.

Eucharist when?

Why is it that the Eucharist has always held such a strong place in the Sunday worship of Christians? The fact that the Eucharist has been the main act of worship every Sunday for most Christians through most of Christian history is incontrovertible. At the Reformation, this came to be widely lost for a variety of reasons, including the new emphasis on the Word as opposed to physical practices. There was also a phenomenon going right back to early centuries of people being reluctant to receive Communion often, for a variety of unsatisfactory reasons. John Chrysostom, in the fifth century, complained regularly to his congregation about it. When after the Reformation you add a weakened sense of the Church and of the Tradition, it is not difficult to understand what happened. The main reformers (Luther, Calvin, Cranmer and others) wanted the Eucharist to be the main service every Sunday, and it was simply through drifting that their original vision was widely lost for so long. Times, however, are changing, and there has been a slow but sure return in recent years, only now again to be undermined by a number of secondary factors—shortage of clergy, higher expectations of worship that are often not met (poor quality in other words), and a lack of grasp of the riches of the Tradition. If a Eucharist is merely trotted out in a routine manner, or is formal where formality doesn't work, people can find more expressive forms of worship more attractive. Often "practices" and "ritual" are associated with formality and soulless routine because of the lack of a trained imagination in those responsible for worship. There are such explanations as these, but why such a divine gift can be sidelined remains ultimately surprising.

Communion

Christianity is more than just a creed—it is *Communion* in God, growing in us, encountered with our eyes and ears and hands and mouths. Of this St Paul says, "The cup of blessing that we bless, is it not *koinonia* (fellowship, communion) in the blood of Christ? The bread that we break, is it not *koinonia* in the body of Christ?" (1 Corinthians 10:16). This is why we call it Holy Communion—a communion with God which also brings us together as people. *Koinonia* has a strong sense of people belonging together, which is why it is sometimes translated "fellowship". Paul goes on to say there is a reason why we, who are many, are one body—the reason is "because there is one bread". So it is often said that the Eucharist manifests the Church, the Eucharist builds the Church, the Eucharist is the supreme place where the Church is at prayer, taken into the communion of the Holy Trinity.

Nothing, of course, is automatic. If you have internalized a traditional understanding of Christian communion, then you can endure a Eucharistic celebration that is done terribly. However, if you are still at the stage of needing to grow in this understanding of communion, more will hang by how well and appropriately it is done. What seems a badly done service can discourage you from continuing. Perhaps there are two questions here: the Christian maturity of each person, and the care and sensitivity with which the Eucharist is celebrated. There is always work to be done on both.

For religious communities, the Eucharist contains and summarizes everything they need. It is all there. On communion, we can say that each religious community lives in communion. Rather than necessarily being deep communication, this communion is more like relationships in the family. Family relationships can be utterly practical and everyday, but in the background there is a tacit knowledge that we belong together, as we have already said. Then, moving on, both in the monastery and in the parish, there is a further dimension, a recognition that this communion is God the Holy Spirit at work, bringing us all, with and in God, to a unity. There is nothing else in the Christian tradition more capable of expressing this, day in and day out, than the Eucharist. No other forms of worship that we can devise can do it. We might think we can do better, and nowadays a lot of energy and imagination is put into trying to do better than the Eucharist; in a subsequent chapter we shall look at what might be going awry when we do that. It depends on what we have set our sights on. If they are set on relationships in the Communion of the Church, then it can only be the Eucharist. For all of us, the Eucharist encapsulates everything we need.

These are big claims to make for something so disarmingly simple—prayers over bread and wine that are then shared. Many things in life are utterly simple but have huge implications: water, singing together, an embrace, two minutes' silence. We could write a long list of such simple things—very simple, but bearing outcomes, meanings, effects, out of all proportion to their simplicity. This should come as no surprise when you begin to examine the hidden hinterlands of practices. Many things are deceptively simple, and the Eucharist is one of them. Below its simplicity a lot takes place. We can include:

- A familiar pattern of prayers and texts, and a patterning of roles (the ancient use of a multiplicity of roles to create a sense of community action is still in the process of being rediscovered in our worship and has yet some way to go).
- Reading of Scripture, some of it in a dramatic mode (e.g. standing for the Gospel, and perhaps a Gospel procession, with candles and servers).
- Prayers for the Church and the world, themselves dramatized by their position in the service.
- The sharing of the Peace.
- Preparation of the table and setting out of bread and wine. This place now becomes the centre of attention. The monastic tradition of a parallel between the altar and the refectory tables, spotlighting the sacred nature of ordinary meals and highlighting the link, is a message for everyone.
- Dialogue between the presider and the people, mirroring the dialogue between Christ and the disciples at the Last Supper, itself following a still-living Jewish tradition.
- The great Thanksgiving (this is what the word Eucharist means) over the bread and wine.

- Within the Thanksgiving, the making memory of God's wonderful deeds in Christ, mentioning specifically at least the incarnation, cross, and resurrection. In particular, the cross and the resurrection resonate through it all.
- The People's Amen—the greatest of all Amens, says St Augustine.
- The receiving of Christ's gifts of his body and blood in bread and wine, very literally the making of Communion, the people often moving bodily to another place in the building.
- Being sent out in the peace of the Lord.

There is no other normal, weekly act of worship where so much is expected to happen, at every level, practical, spiritual, aesthetic, Church-wise (ecclesiologically). This last word points back to the Eucharist making the Church, manifesting the Church, showing what it truly is. Everything is there, not just for the life of monks and nuns, but for us all. This disarmingly simple and jejune practice has more to it the closer you look. It certainly takes us into the realm of the imagination, and whatever help we may get from analysing what the Eucharist is about, we still need to take our feet off the ground and fly in order to get at the heart of it. Gregory Dix, in his ecumenically acclaimed *Shape of the Liturgy*, puts it very finely, in a passage which is often quoted, but never wears thin:

> Was ever another command so obeyed? For century after century, spreading slowly to every continent and country and among every race on earth, this action has been done, in every conceivable human circumstance, for every conceivable human need from infancy and before it to extreme old age and after it, from the pinnacles of earthly greatness to the refuge of fugitives in the caves and dens of the earth ... while the lions roared in the nearby amphitheatre; on the beach at Dunkirk; while the hiss of scythes in the thick June grass came faintly through the windows of the church; tremulously, by an old monk on the fiftieth anniversary of his vows; furtively, by an exiled bishop who had hewn timber all day in a prison camp near Murmansk; gorgeously, for the canonization of S. Joan of Arc—one could fill many pages with the reasons why [people] have done this, and not

tell a hundredth part of them. And best of all, week by week and
month by month, on a hundred thousand successive Sundays,
faithfully, unfailingly, across all the parishes of Christendom, the
pastors have done this just to make ... the holy common people
of God.[19]

Daily Prayer

Pride of place also belongs to another item in the Christian treasure-
house alongside the Eucharist: the practice of keeping in touch with God
every day. "Pray without ceasing" (1 Thessalonians 5:17), "pray always"
(Luke 18:1). Through Christian history this has crystallized around short
daily services offered in church, especially in the morning and evening.
Hand-in-hand with those there have always been ways of praying on
your own or in the family. Contemporary interest in Britain in Celtic
Christianity has made known, for instance, a practice of prayers said
when doing routine tasks during the day like lighting the fire or cooking
a meal. Daily praying has been in fact a normal part of most religions
from the earliest beginnings, and it can be seen alive and well among
many Muslims today. Every parish is called to be a place of prayer, a
praying community, but what is the situation today? Daily services of
prayer happen in convents and monasteries, but they got the idea from
the earliest "parishes". Other communities, like cathedrals, also have these
services every day, and some parishes do. There are also many clergy who
celebrate these services in small groups or alone, and some lay people use
them in one adapted form or another. One of the great things about this
is the sense of praying with the whole Church, either at the same time
of day, or with similar words, or both. There is a sense of this being the
prayer of everybody who makes up the Church. Not everyone, however,
is able to do this sort of thing, either because of time, personal situation,
or just lack of attraction. There is, however, a rich tradition of all kinds of
simpler forms of prayer offered with the whole Church, and we need to be
rediscovering them and evolving new forms of them suitable for our time.

---

[19]   Gregory Dix, *The Shape of the Liturgy* (London: Dacre Press, 1945), p. 744.

In the Roman Catholic Church, the Daily Prayer services became a privatized preserve of the clergy, who would sit (or walk up and down) reciting them quietly. Not everywhere, however: they survived as public worship in cathedrals and large churches for a long time in many countries, and a lot has been done over recent years to return these offices to their place in every Christian's journey with God. In the churches of the Reformation, there has been some rediscovery, but there is a long way to go. Anglicanism has a unique history of public daily offices, of which I have outlined a history in my book *Company of Voices*,[20] but the question of how this tradition can be lived by the people of God today remains unfinished business.

The internet

An abundance of resources is available on the internet in both websites and apps, and these are widely used. The Church of England website offers a fourfold choice each day: the texts of the Daily Offices, or a choral performance, or a choral performance of a simplified office, or simply a collect prayer for each day. Many of the resources on the internet are unfortunately very individualistic ("me and my prayer"), which is of course an important part of the Christian life, but not so helpful in taking us out of ourselves and rooting us in the Church. There need to be more apps available that put that right.

One area for exploration is corporate use of the internet—groups gathering to use these resources together, forms of worship which put people in touch with each other (my own community's streamed services have created an online congregation who communicate with each other often while the service is going on), and parish apps which bring everybody together as a parish. Live streaming, despite the drawbacks, is here to stay, and has opened up opportunities not there before, as well as telephoned daily services that have become established in some places. We obviously should grasp this opportunity and make good use of people who have the ability to develop resources and approaches. The challenge will be how to hold all

---

20   George Guiver, *Company of Voices* (Norwich: Canterbury Press, 2001).

this variety of approaches and content together, for if ways of praying are being made more easily available, more people will hopefully be coming to prayer; but if it takes the form of a free-for-all marketplace, prayer will always be firing on less than four cylinders. Is the parish the right place to start a renewal? One problem is that local experiments are isolated, not universal, and therefore not supported from outside. The spur provided by a sense that this is what the whole Church does is missing: the very nature of the thing lies in its being an act of the whole Church. The individual attempt of one parish to engage in Daily Prayer together is for this reason in a weak position.

Daily Prayer in parishes

I have helped with experiments in a variety of parishes trying to find simple forms of office that people could happily use. They became simpler and simpler, until a final experiment simply provided a collect for each day, but never have these experiments got very far. In the course of them I have found it difficult to persuade congregations that prayer is part of their corporate calling, something to practise day in and day out with this corporate sense; it is difficult for us to take to heart that while the feel of it may vary and sometimes it may feel empty, nevertheless it is to be trusted to bear long-term fruits for me and everyone with whom I am bound up if I persevere. It may be that we have to accept that some of us are content simply to pray in church on Sundays. Nowadays we cannot see the point of doing things just because they are there to be done.

At every stage, some people were helped in these parish experiments, and some may well still be using the forms we developed, but I came to realize that tinkering with the content was not enough: in the end you cannot just use the *form* of worship to generate commitment. There needs to be something there in the person for the form to hook onto. This raises a question: why is it difficult for so many people to pray and to worship with dedicated, sustained commitment, and with a sense of doing this together as a community?

The hump

The German writer Romano Guardini in 1964 asked a famous question which has echoed down the decades in the study of Christian worship: "Are modern people any longer capable of worship?" (German: *liturgiefähig*). Although numbers of people still go to church, the overall mindset in our society is not at all in tune with the Church, and God and worship are widely regarded as irrelevant. Many minds have tried to make sense of this, and we can't simply produce a solution out of our hats; but in order to put our minds to the subject of prayer, practices and the Church, it will help to take a look at various things about modern people, including ourselves.

Firstly, we can fail to recognize what a different world we live in compared with not so long ago. The world for us now is **disenchanted**— whether you practise a religion or not, it is rare for any of us to believe in witches, wizards, fairies or magic. This is a big change arising from about the seventeenth century. It has not removed the foundation for Christian belief and practice—if it had done, nobody would be going to church any more. The former enchanted picture of the world, however, used to nudge people in God's direction, and that nudge has been taken away. It was an unsatisfactory nudge, better done without, but its disappearance has put Christians more on their mettle (which is good for them of course). It now takes more effort to think in terms of unseen realities. While many people are still able to be confident Christians in a disenchanted world, for people who were never very committed, the de-magicking of the world has left their weak faith without something that had functioned as a significant prop, and they have melted away. In the middle are many who go to church because the worship is a help but find it less easy to become passionate about it. Three sorts of people: those who still happily believe and commit themselves, those who have melted away, and in the middle the many churchgoers who are iffy about unseen things.

Another way the world has changed is that in the past, many elements in people's lives were knitted together. You went to church; the church provided a social world and clubs for young people and adults; it was a focus for people's financial giving, a source of music and art and outings, permeating many aspects of life in the congregation and the public forum. For all of us, that composite thing has **broken up**. We might go to church, but our social life, our support for charities and service of our neighbour, all tend to be in separate, usually secular, areas. The same thing has happened to the family, its members tending to pursue disparate interests with perhaps separate timetables, resulting in dispersal of the life of the home. The church has become something you dip into, or hover near the edge of, at somewhere less than a burning commitment.

We are also of course more **individual**, more independent-minded, and less equipped to build community. Standing like this in an individual space leaves us with the feeling that my world and my picture of the world are what ultimately matters. I am me, and from this standpoint inside my head I look out onto the church as something over there that I am trying to assess. That puts up a curtain—it might be the finest of curtains, but it is sufficient to enable us to feel that it all starts and ends with me. The church and its life and worship are now more like a TV programme that I choose to watch or switch off, rather than something I LIVE with the whole of myself.

Yet another way that life has changed for all of us concerns what Charles Taylor has called our "social imaginary".[21] You could say this boils down to a **common sense** that we all share, a feel for the mentality of our society, a shared picture of what is normal behaviour and what makes sense. It produces in us, he says, *deep normative images*. This "social imaginary" that has grown up has been fashioned by our secular, scientific world, which puts God as far as it can out of sight. This "social imaginary" is in all of us, whether we like it or not. The modern world is in our veins, in the air we breathe; it has made us what we are, right from when we were born, and it brings with it a marginalizing of God. This will tend to make our faith that bit more faltering, uncertain, lacking in confidence. For Peter Berger, the effect is a feeling that religious practice has less **plausibility**.[22] Some things in our society are plausible, while for some other things, like religion, their plausibility is, well, not rock-solid.

---

[21] Charles Taylor, *A Secular Age* (Cambridge, MA: Harvard University Press, 2007), pp. 159ff.

[22] See Peter Berger, *The Sacred Canopy* (Garden City, NY: Doubleday, 1967).

This is such an important phenomenon that we will look at it more closely in a separate chapter.

Then there is **science**. The popular supposition that science disproves religion is very much around, despite all evidence to the contrary, not least the fact that many scientists are Christians, and that theology itself is a science that uses the same practices as the people in white coats in laboratories. What is more insidious and undermining, however, is the sense that we have become so clever and capable that we feel we can do anything. Everything now is possible, and so God seems that much less special than he used to seem. We are in charge, and despite ongoing difficulties, we are perfectly capable of taking the world by the scruff of the neck and doing what we want with it. Just give us time.

Then there is what you might call **naturalism**. We have faith in things being what they naturally are; we feel it important that people should be "authentic" rather than trying to be what they are not; we are a very informal society, in clothes and social behaviour, even in worlds like politics or the Church. We are not on the whole happy with routine, with ritual, with formal behaviour—we want to be able to be "natural". This is in all of us, and is largely to be welcomed: it is good to be free from pomposity, stuffiness, mindless routine and doing the "done thing". However, it has brought with it a superficial attitude to rituals and formal behaviour. Much has been written on ritual and symbol in recent years, enough to show both how important they are for us and how much they are still there in our lives, widely unrecognized. Mary Douglas said that we live in an "anti-ritual society".[23] If this is so, we are going to have difficulty in persuading people to do the practices of the Christian faith day in and day out, trusting them to be a pathway that in the longer term will take us towards growth in the faith.

"Why," people may ask, "should we bother anyway?" We have all been changed by the new and widespread prosperity of our times. A large proportion of us, despite grumblings, have in fact all we need—we have **no need** for God. Why should we bother? Perhaps that may be a contributory factor, but there are also, shamefully for our society, large

---

[23]   Mary Douglas, *Natural Symbols*, 2nd edn (London: Routledge, 1996), Chapter 1.

numbers of the hidden poor: they do not have all they need, and they don't turn to God either. The two are affected by how God is perceived in our culture. There are, however, questions to be asked about why "the poor" would not have the courage to get in contact with Christian communities and parishes. It may be that the people who have all they need don't sense a need of God, while those who don't have enough have problems relating to the Church, or don't even think of trying to relate to it. The Church is assumed to be alien. This suggests that in trying to find ways of enabling our society to come to faith, we need to be careful not simply to have in our sights those who have enough; we need also to be examining how the poor can expect an open-armed welcome, a theme rightly highlighted by Pope Francis.

These are some of the things that can make us ask if our society is any longer capable of worship. For myself, it is clear that all of them, and other things about ourselves which have not been mentioned, do not in any way amount to a death warrant for life with God. They are, rather, a **hump**. Humps are needless obstacles that have to be got over. We saw an example in Chapter 4, where two groups of people (for and against Donald Trump) had pictures of each other that made them passionate enemies, but once someone had the courage patiently to bring them together, the hump was miraculously overcome, and people even began to make friendships despite deep divisions. With regard to faith, we need to ask more questions about the nature of the intractable hump that keeps people from God, or keeps people from solid commitment.

Light from the monastery

What light can religious communities throw for us here? In them, anyone can see that a strongly shaped life of prayer and worship is perfectly possible for modern people. Religious sisters and brothers are all children of our time, and we bring our society with us. In my community, for instance, the timetable described in Chapter 2, with all its regular prayer times consisting of familiar texts and music, for us is simply there—we do it because we do it. Some of us are very free modern spirits, yet it still works.

Religious communities are first of all a sign to the modern Church that it is perfectly possible to respond to the New Testament call to pray always. If it can work for us, it is difficult to say such a strong pattern of prayer practices no longer makes sense in our contemporary culture. For religious brothers and sisters, the times of prayer "work": they inculcate a prayerful frame of mind, and prayer becomes part of the landscape. Jesus cautioned us against empty repetitions, and he went on to teach us a repetition that isn't empty: the Lord's Prayer. He then left it to us to expand on the example given. Secondly, religious communities are there to accompany the Church in its prayer, to give everyone a leg-up, and it is good for communities in return to know they are accompanied. One Syrian monk has said that in his own Christian culture "the monastery is the parish's muscles". Since the beginning of the pandemic, many people have discovered to their surprise the effect of regularly tuning in to the Daily Prayer of religious communities. It does something to you. That something may perhaps have a place in the parish.

If religious communities come over as normal to people that encounter them, and are a strong public sign of the perfect believability of Christian faith in our world, there are many lay people and clergy who are also as "normal" as anybody else in our society and give clear demonstration that all the problems I have listed above as the "hump" are no automatic death warrant for faith. It is simply that these Christians are the other side of the hump. How can we help the world to come over to the other side? It is a huge question, of course, and many are wrestling with it. While there can be no simple answer, there are things that stand out, and among them I put forward here a scheme to help people give themselves to the Eucharist and Daily Prayer.

From world to Church to God

The New Testament depicts a faith that appeals to people's passions and their gut instincts. Following Christ has to be passionate, even if we are British people, for passion in this sense can be either full on, as they say in South America, or understated. If I look all around me, I see a world in turmoil and a Church without wind in its sails. It is not enough for the

Church to want to be at the service of others without thought for itself. That is fine for each of its members, but not for the Church, which is the Body of Christ. We cannot serve others without thought for Christ. We have to have thought for the Church. But the wellbeing of the Church does relate to the wellbeing of those it is called to serve—the Church is not an end in itself. Here we have a message: look at the state of the world with all its conflicts, sufferings and needs; such a world needs a Church that is strong. It is the world's loss where the Church is weak. How may the Church be strong? We are not talking here about strength in numbers, finance, influence or power. Our strength is made known in our weakness in such things. What we are to be strong in is our faith. "Keep alert, stand firm in your faith, be courageous, be strong" (1 Corinthians 16:13). "Be strong in the Lord and in the strength of his power. Put on the whole armour of God, so that you may be able to stand . . . " (Ephesians 6:10–11). The world needs a Church that is strong, and it can only be strong by walking as closely as possible with God. The message here for Christians is: look at the world and the mess it is in, and then at the current decline of the Church—here is a clarion call to do something to enable the Church to be a strong presence, strong in the one thing necessary, which is God. For that it needs to be a people that prays, living in our lives the Lord's cross and resurrection through our Baptism, and the Eucharist and Daily Prayer. A people strengthened in those things will be more likely to feel impelled to service and to mission. Among all the approaches that need to be explored in order to help each other over the "hump", this message is at least self-evident and has a logic capable of spurring us on.

The parish's prayer

We are still faced with my problem that in reality it is difficult for many people today to take on a commitment to Daily Prayer. In Luke 16, Jesus surprisingly commends a crafty manager who told a man who owed 100 jugs of oil to give just 50 and call it quits. It is one of those rum stories that make us scratch our chins, but the principle is good, because it is realistic. This parable provides St Benedict with one of the most important principles in his Rule: whatever is asked of anybody should be a close enough fit to who they actually are. The Abbot therefore has to be prepared to adapt the Rule to what the person is cut out for. That gives me an idea for one possible way of a parish sustaining a daily offering of prayer. The parish decides to set up a network. All effective bandwagons need a name, so for the purpose of this discussion let's call it *In Touch*. This will be a network for keeping us in touch with each other, in touch with the world, and in touch with God. It brings together in a common effort many things that are happening separately: people saying their private prayers, clergy saying or singing the offices in church, groups praying together, people following prayer apps on their phones, small groups in care homes getting together to pray each day, busy folk who can't screw themselves up to pray regularly, but can light daily a tealight on the window ledge, setting a flag flying for God, those who go into church to light a candle, people studying their Bible, those taking the sacraments to the sick, people living alone joining in in simple ways. All of these and more are simply regarded as practices plugged in to *In Touch*. Communications can include requests for prayer and simple reports on the network, as well as concerns for the wider world, and there may be a noticeboard available in the parish newsletter and also an app. There will be people who only pray, say, on Sundays, and that is OK, but they can still be part of *In Touch*. Dioceses and other local units could have their own versions. It may be that such a flexible network approach would be closer to what both St Benedict and St Luke are intimating; but part of the point of the whole thing is that all the threads are drawn together and given a name. Such a connecting-up of scattered bits and pieces may well help our travailing world to have a stronger Church in its midst, a Church strong in prayer and in belonging.

This consideration of Christian practices began by looking at Baptism, the Eucharist and Daily Prayer, and it has put a finger on an elephant in the room, which is the obstacles that modern society throws in our path. Putting that on one side for a moment, there are more Christian practices we first need to look at.

7

More practices

It would be interesting to know what the response would be if, in our attempts to evangelize the world, we stopped trying so hard to get people to believe, and instead offered them training in Christian practices. This will seem less off-beam the closer we look at it. In the previous chapter, we gave our attention to Baptism, the Eucharist and Daily Prayer. It was important to start there, but there is a range of other things we now need to give attention to, and the first of these is love and service of our neighbour.

At the service of others

A wonderful, mixed and hoary introduction to the spirit of monastic life is found in what is now often referred to as *The Sayings of the Desert Fathers*.[24] These desert monks and nuns of the fourth to the sixth centuries put surprising emphasis on loving our neighbour, and often do it with an entertaining and provocative clarity. When you read these stories, you gain the overwhelming impression that a top priority of monastic life was loving the brothers and sisters. So, for example, we read: "Abbot John the Dwarf said, 'A house is not built by beginning at the top and working down. You must begin with the foundations in order to reach the top.' They said to him, 'What does this saying mean?' He said, 'The foundation is our neighbour, whom we must win, and that is the place to begin. For all the commandments of Christ depend on this one.'" This

---

[24]   Benedicta Ward (ed.), *The Sayings of the Desert Fathers* (Kalamazoo. MI: Cistercian, 2004).

echoes the first letter of St John, who says, "If someone does not love their neighbour whom they have seen, they cannot love God whom they have not seen" (1 John 4:20). The proof of the pudding is in the eating. Loving and serving our neighbour cannot just remain an attitude: it is a *practice* of Christianity. Although we began with Baptism, Eucharist and Daily Prayer, they are useless without this. They need to go hand in hand with it from the start, and if you start with one rather than the other, it can only be with love of neighbour, as Abbot John rightly says.

Over the subsequent centuries, one way this establishes itself is in monastic hospitality: provision in most communities is made for receiving guests to enable them to share a little in the life. They are to be treated with love and respect. Sometimes people come in a situation of need—every now and again, for instance, communities can be asked to take in someone who has hit a snag in their life, say someone on remand. Whatever they are accused of doing, whoever they might have hurt, they are always received with love and respect, because all are sinners, and we are in no position to sit in judgement on anybody. It is enough that the person is a human being in a fix. Religious communities also always get caught up with the human life around them—situations crop up of every kind, people come with all manner of needs, and life in its variety is always impinging. As far as its capabilities will allow, a community will respond as Christians should. In addition, it is normal for communities in one way or another to roll their sleeves up for others. There are communities dedicated to particular forms of ministry, many of them among the poor and needy. My own community, in its work in Africa, found itself thrown into a kaleidoscope of practices, from accompanying people in their sufferings and tragedies, to taking part in the struggle against injustice, to unexpected activities like pulling teeth.

This service of neighbour depends on neighbourly love, not simply as an attitude, but as action—love of your neighbour shows itself in what you do, first of all, rather than in what you think. It grows through chemistry with the gospel, and so needs to be backed up by prayer and reflection, and often some training—not necessarily in things like pulling teeth, but certainly in grasping how the whole spectrum of the gospel fits together. We are not talking about serving my neighbour in one department of my life and going to church in another. How do they fit together and fertilize each other? Trained reflection on life with our neighbour cannot but help us grow in prayer and in appreciation of the Eucharist and the Church. St Benedict recognized that we all need training in making these connections—even though his Rule was written for monks and nuns, he still felt the need to remind everybody that every visitor to the monastery is Christ becoming present.[25]

Many church members will struggle with the idea of Christ being in members of the congregation, and may need to be told you don't need to feel it—it's not about how they affect you, but how you see them and behave towards them, how you practise it. Sunday worship can seem to have little practical connection with putting love into action, even though that may be going on, a lot or a little, in our secular lives. And yet there are many ways that worship will benefit if we are thinking of everybody else there. There is plenty to do, even in our own congregations, if communication is good enough for us to know what is needed. Often it isn't. Many people slip in and out of church without finding the courage to pour out what weighs them down. A friend of mine once told me of a chap called Joe who was in church every week but didn't easily mix with people. He got to know Joe and started having him round to meals now and again. Joe's marriage had broken up, and it was difficult living on his own. When my friend mentioned him to people in the congregation and to the priest, no one could identify who he was talking about. Later, Joe stopped coming, and after a while my friend decided to seek out a pub on the other side of town which he knew Joe frequented, to try and find out where he lived. There he was told that Joe was ill and had stopped coming. A little more detective work enabled him to be tracked down, and my friend found Joe alone and ill in bed. It emerged that he would like to receive Communion. My friend reported this to the priest and other parish officers, but nobody ever went. It is important in our congregations that we look out for each other. Loving our neighbour is not simply a principle to be trotted out, it is a practice, not just between individuals, but fr the Church's engagement with our society.

---

[25]   Rule of St Benedict, 53.1

Teaching and help about mutual obedience

In an earlier chapter, we talked about mutual submission. This too is an attitude, but first of all it is a practice. It may start with individuals working at it, but then gradually, ideally, it becomes part of the culture of a community. A sustained attitude of mutual respect and due humility in response to what comes from others is not easy in our culture, where self-assertion can be seen as a virtue. Having the courage of our convictions is a fine thing, but occasions when it should be needed are not normally frequent. When in Ephesians 5:21 we are told, "Submit yourselves one to another", this is not a call to be a doormat: it is a call to be realistic, not carried away with our own view of things, but to be open to different views. The way it often works out in religious communities of brothers and sisters is in the form of patience—a trained habit of being quick to listen and slow to speak. In any disagreements or discussion of contrasting options, the approach will be to give it time—let the other person feel they have been listened to, and you are halfway to a solution. Once in my community we came to a big sticking-point in discussing a difficult matter and didn't know what to do—we were divided down the middle. We asked, "What would Christine and Martin, our facilitators, get us to do?" We dreamed up a process which involved the following: brothers went off in pairs, and each wrote down what he thought and read it out to the other. There was no discussion. The twos came together in fours and did a similar exercise in response to specific questions. The fours came together in two groups of eight, where all could say what they wanted, but there was no discussion. Then we all came together as 16 brothers and went round the room, each saying what he thought at this point. We then had a vote, and it was unanimous. This outcome made very clear to us something that we had already learned from our facilitators: free discussion can sometimes be unhelpful and even damaging; instead, it can be incredibly helpful to do an exercise where the discussion is tightly channelled, in such a way that everyone feels they have had their say and that they have been listened to. That is one of the most important things you can achieve in any group discussion, that everyone feels they have been heard.

Mutual submission is scattered all through the teaching of Jesus and spelled out more specifically in the Epistles. It is one of the building blocks of unity, and without it conflict becomes easier. It would be good to find ways of referring to it (and St Benedict puts some of this well) when meetings are held, when groups deal with business, and wherever each of us can feel inclined to defend our patch. The business we are about is discerning the will of God, and imitating John the Baptist, one of the inspirers of monasticism: "I must decrease that Christ might increase." This mutual submission is a *practice* in the first instance, but if it goes in the right direction, it will move more and more towards a culture of corporate charity and attention.

Patience

Monastic life is tested most by the very people who make it up. Living with these people is the work of a lifetime—religious communities work at the coalface of human nature in a way that is not usual, and this tends to produce a certain kind of person, a particular kind of group. The life tends to cultivate a patient, attentive disposition that gives at least a bit more space to others (we must not claim too much, but this much is fair to say). Such a community's life distances itself from a quick-acting world that wants to take all problems by the scruff of the neck, and a hyperactive Church tempted to see that as the only way of tackling things. This can make religious communities difficult and even exasperating to work with—if a building project is going on, for instance, architects and builders can need quick decisions, but they may need to wait until the next meeting of the Chapter, and the Chapter may conclude that more time is needed to reflect further, and so it goes on. In the long run, nothing is lost, but everything needs to be approached with patience, and this is inseparable from mutual submission and listening.

Imaginative use of the church
building and special places

One practice central to most religions is having special places. Church buildings are mentioned more than once in this book as important "practices" for living the gospel. The idealism that has risen up since the 1960s has rightly sought to overcome notions of the sacred as representing a world set apart, sealed off from everyday life in a "sacred" place of its own, as if it were compensating for an absence of God in daily life. Celebrations of the Eucharist have come into secular spaces and people's homes, and at the same time practices and events of ordinary life have come into church buildings. In right measure, this has brought a breath of fresh air, and also given us new eyes to see the presence of Christ in the ordinary.

There are two possible long-term consequences to this approach: one is that you set a low value on the church building and say the gospel is really above such things. Christ is in real life, not shut away in shrines. The result is a takeover by ordinary everyday life, as the church building becomes like any other place, or is abandoned. The second possibility is that the church building continues to be valued highly, precisely because of its chemistry with the secular world we live in. This sort of chemistry happens when two different things meet, both of them highly charged. You come off the street, push open the door and go in. Let Philip Larkin's poem "Church Going" take over here:

... though I've no idea
What this accoutred frowsty barn is worth,
It pleases me to stand in silence here;
A serious house on serious earth it is,
In whose blent air all our compulsions meet,
Are recognised, and robed as destinies.
And that much never can be obsolete,
Since someone will forever be surprising
A hunger in himself to be more serious,
And gravitating with it to this ground,
Which, he once heard, was proper to grow wise in . . . [26]

I spoke in an earlier chapter of how religious communities often see themselves as holding a piece of ground for God: life is lived there in such a way that the feel of the place contrasts with the world of those entering through the gate—there is a climate that greets us and takes us where we hadn't expected to go. This is equally true of parish churches and cathedrals: many people can testify, perhaps to their surprise, to Larkin's experience. The encounter of holy places with our secular society can arouse powerful responses. There is a growing interest in the importance of "place" in human life, and especially in religions. A General Synod report on the matter has drawn attention to this, finding its basis in the incarnation, and likening the church building to the particularity of place and time that Jesus came into.[27]

We can take this further and look to our understanding of what a human being is. It is our nature to create special places. "Place" functions for us as an extension of our bodies. A normal home is that too, all put together by this instinctive desire. Religious communities need their home and their church or chapel. There are exceptional groups of brothers and sisters who lead a simple life and celebrate Mass on a kitchen table—nothing is absolute—but they are the exception that

---

[26] Philip Larkin, "Church Going", in *The Less Deceived* (London: Marvell Press, 1955), p. 87.

[27] General Synod Report by the Church Buildings Review Group, *GS 2008*, 2015.

proves the rule. A congregation may worship in its church hall while repairs are being done, and find it refreshing, but it does not take long for people to be keen to get back into church. We can only conclude that church buildings are nothing less than a key part of the gospel. It is possible to do without them, but not for long. It is not possible not to want them or benefit from them. Christ came to human beings as they really are, and our instinct for special buildings and special places is an unavoidable part of the actual humanity he came amongst. It is simply how we are. We can therefore say that using church buildings, going in them to pray, arranging and decorating them, using them as witnesses of God for mission, are part of the range of Christian practices which we do well to make the most of.

Music, singing, art, the imagination

"I came that they may have life, and have it abundantly" (John 10:10). The gospel is about being human beings fully alive. There are significant ways in which our wings are clipped to prevent this today. To begin with, people don't sing. Singing is beneficial for body and mind—a way of coming alive with the whole of ourselves. Teaching people to sing, and to have the confidence to sing in community, needs to be part of the Church's mission, if we are calling people to be full human beings. It would be good to find ways of training Christians in this fundamental human practice. Cathedrals could have a role here, and musicians in the congregation, and suitable people could be given training, for them in their turn to train the congregation to sing. A lot more could be done with our music-making if we have the will. Mike Leigh, a priest and former opera singer, writes:

> For many years I have championed the use of simple unaccompanied songs both within liturgical settings and in other areas of ministry . . . we call this 'natural voice singing' or 'paper-less song', as it requires no paper for words or music or instruments and so it is a natural way to sing together . . . I recently came across . . . the Natural Voice Network, which is

a UK-based organization that links community song leaders around the country using this type of music . . . can we create a Christian community based on song? In other words, can we create a Church that meets just to sing, and through the communal activity of singing together, experience the living God in deep and profound ways? This question takes us deeper, to a place where singing is the foundation of the community and leads us to a sacramental encounter with the living God . . . To explore this further I have been gathering a few people just to sing together and see what happens, and we meet regularly now . . . What we discover when we sing together is that we are far more engaged with each other than when we are in church on a Sunday morning, and we are also much more sensitive to each other's needs and concerns. We also discover that we are more spiritually connected . . . [28]

We need to be helped out of deep assumptions that singing isn't for us, or that we can't do it. It is part of everyone's birthright.

The visual arts are another obvious form of Christian practice: in all their manifestations they have gained an important place in our society, and the growing interest in them in churches is encouraging, but slow and patchy. It is surprising what can come out of people if they have the opportunity to engage with art and meet artists. It would also benefit the Church's credibility for congregations to rise to higher artistic standards in the design and decoration of churches, and how things are arranged in them (can't we become less make-do and take more care?). Going to church should in either rich or simple ways always be a visual treat.

The same goes for drama—making use of actors, and of their ability to encourage ordinary people to learn what they can do in acting, can be transformative. I once went to a church where the Gospel was silently mimed by a group of people before it was read, and this had the effect of making the reading more powerful, and furthermore fired up the reader

---

[28] Mike Leigh, "Singing for the Soul: the joy of singing together", *Quarterly Review, Community of the Resurrection Mirfield* 468 (2020), pp. 13–17.

(who happened to be me), who was very affected by the mime. Our imaginations need to be set going, and it is so easily done.

Practising community

Something of particular interest is a new tendency towards communities, usually non-resident, that live a range of aspects of the monastic life. People, ordained and lay, in many walks of life, are choosing to live with commitments to community, Daily Offices, and living under a rule; they normally live individually, but their communities bring members together as often as they can for days spent together. This is often referred to under the umbrella term "New Monasticism".[29] It is sometimes remarked that these communities are enabling something which the parish is now failing to provide. I have heard this said about parishes in various countries of the Western world. Recently in discussion with some French Roman Catholics exactly the same thing was said: many people are finding the parish is not providing what they are seeking. This is not a judgement on parishes and their clergy, but simply an indication of what they are up against. "New Monasticism" in its ideal conception is a strong form of something that is happening in many ways in the Church: a quest for forms of committed communities and groups, some of whom would have a place within the life of a parish, while others are more dispersed, perhaps in some form of association with a traditional religious community. Particularly within the climate of modern society, living a Christian life can need some form of scaffolding in addition to the normal life of a parish as it is at the moment. Perhaps "New Monasticism" has a role in working towards "new parish".

---

[29] See, for instance, Graham Cray, Ian Mobsby and Aaron Kennedy (eds), *New Monasticism as Fresh Expression of Church* (Norwich: Canterbury Press, 2011); Matthew Bullimore and Sarah Coakley, *The Vowed Life* (Norwich: Canterbury Press, 2023), Chapter 8.

Practices of prayer

Christians' prayer has over the centuries given birth to a rich range of physical prayer practices: the Rosary, prayer ropes, holding crosses, lighting candles, *Lectio divina*, prayer stools, icons, prayer notes, visiting the church building, corporate silence, and much more, and our highly imaginative generation has the gifts to develop others that are good for our time. Then there is prayer with the body: the sign of the cross, in which we identify ourselves with Christ crucified, kneeling, bowing, raising our hands. Some practices almost overlap with dance, like the lesser and greater prostrations practised by the Eastern Orthodox, which also incidentally give good exercise to the body. Then there are practices in and out of the liturgy at different seasons of the year, such as the foot-washing on Maundy Thursday, coming to the Cross on Good Friday, confession to a priest and the weight-lifting blessing of absolution, corporate practices like quiet days, going on pilgrimage, Stations of the Cross. This panoply contributes to a silent working in our inner selves, and also in our bodies and muscles, just as in ballroom dancing. Such a range of things can develop innate "skills" in us.

It is important to ask, who is doing all of this? We tend to think of the individual, but there is always a corporate element to being Christians, and all Christian forms of prayer have this about them, that they sit within a universal framework before a personal one. In my visits to Romania, I have been impressed by the role that prayer practices play in the formation of Christians, and so I wrote to Fr Dan Sandu, a Romanian Orthodox priest, to ask him about their practices. His reply included the following:

> Each time I speak to people in confession, I encourage them to pray together, even when the children are very small, so that they can get used to prayer before they understand its meaning. Some people really do it: they pray together, sing a psalm or a hymn, forgive each other before going to bed.
>
> ... I was brought up in a family of six children, all of us in two rooms ... When we started, one by one, leaving the parental home, all the others felt like mourning with sadness and cried.

Now, when my boy left our home for the UK, we did not feel any longer the same, as he had spent so much time in his own room of the house, or in the city with his friends, and we only saw each other over dinner, the only compulsory family activity. As for my childhood, I will never forget the prayer corner in our small rural house, with Christ's icon hanging in the corner ... where my mother used to put all of us to prayer, kneeling down, and then to bed (two beds for six children). Of course, we did not fall asleep very soon, and I saw every single evening my father and mother praying in the same way before the icon of Christ after finishing the tidying of the house. That corner was indeed the "holy place", the corner of hope, the corner of salvation. In my child's mind, there was no safer place like that in the world.

Here we see a moving picture of prayer in the family that engages our whole humanity, and the setting of the home, and we get a glimpse too of how the modern world is eroding such possibilities. There is a need to be countercultural, but how far is that feasible in such a world? There is a practice in this area which I call "trusting perseverance".

Trusting perseverance

In a religious community, life is full of practices of all kinds, and you can't drop out of them. We are committed together, and we do them, however we feel. This could lead to the life feeling oppressive, frustrating or even downright loony; on the whole it doesn't, because over the years you learn to see more and more the fruits of a perseverance in trusting these well-tried practices. Outside the supportive framework of life in a religious community, this will be a hard call for anyone today. Let me illustrate this from my own experience. When I am away from the Community, especially for an extended period such as the annual holiday, I light a candle in front of an icon and sing the Daily Offices as we do at home, though normally saying the Psalms rather than singing them. I hear the sound of my own voice, and it feels disconcertingly as if I am the centre of attention. I plough on, and after a day or two that fades away, it becomes less self-conscious, and I have a sense of offering the liturgy of the Church. However, I find, particularly in the parts that I don't sing but say, that the usual stray thoughts come in, like, "What am I going to have for breakfast?" More than that, however, there is a little whirlpool of other feelings going on, a mixture of thoughts such as, "Aren't I good to be doing this?"; "Aren't I impressive in the way I'm doing it?"; "Aren't I concentrating too much on my performance rather than on God?" After years of this, I am used to it, and just let it go on. All these involuntary bubble-ups lead me to a powerful awareness of everything being the other way up. It is not me trying to do a thing; it is God doing the thing and letting me in on it. Christ is lifting me up into Evensong, or whichever the office is. I feel lifted up as if in a basket into the office that is going on. Although I fish and fumble about with inappropriate thoughts, that is like the dust being shaken off a mop. The reality does not sit in me myself but in the practice. The reality is in the candle, the icon, the divine words, the singing, the gestures. By the end, I can feel I have encountered God, but even more there is a sense of having been found. Trusting perseverance is not so much about finding qualities within ourselves—it is more about giving ourselves to Christian pathways that have proved they can be trusted.

This is one of the most difficult messages of this book for contemporary people. My experience of many visits to Romania has left me with a powerful sense of the fruits of simply doing things because that is what we do. It has little to do with our feelings at the time, or what we hope to get out of it—it is simply getting on and doing something with our body and putting the prima donna in our head in its place. And somewhere in it all there actually grows a love of the things.

St Benedict says in his rule with a cheeky dash of humour, "We read that monks should not drink wine at all, but since the monks of our own day cannot be persuaded of this, let us at least agree to drink moderately, and not to the point of excess, for wine makes even wise men go astray".[30] Just as his Italian monks could not be persuaded not to drink wine, we could also say that trusting perseverance in practices is what we need, but no one in our own day can be persuaded of it. Perhaps we should at this point take a look at its opposite.

---

[30]   Rule of St Benedict, 40.6f.

8

Going for effect

In my community, it is the custom that the Superior, the head of the Community, normally chairs all meetings as well as committees. Our college once set up a working group for a particular matter, consisting of myself (at that time the Superior), another brother, a bishop, and a businessman. I opened with a prayer, and then proceeded to chair the meeting. After a minute or two, someone politely coughed and pointed out that for this working group the bishop was the chair of the meeting. With the best grace I could muster, I duly handed over to His Grace. As we all knew each other well, this was simply amusing, but there are situations where grabbing the leadership might be more tricky. A rigged election in a dictatorship, for instance, where the obvious winner is declared the loser. Or rich people deciding from on high what would be good for poor people. Dictators are fully aware of what they are doing, but my two other examples show a state of unawareness—taking the reins, having assumed without good reason that we are in charge. Backseat driving is another instance. The person at the wheel is in charge, but a passenger keeps telling them what to do, perhaps not fully aware of themselves while they do it.

Monastic life has stringent safeguards against this streak in human nature. If you want to do something in the library or the kitchen, you first ask the brother or sister in charge. If you see something lying around, you think twice before clearing it away. Many a frustrated sister or brother has left a door propped open while they fetch a heavy object and, staggering back breathlessly with the unwieldy burden, arrive to find the door has "helpfully" been shut; or they have left a dustpan for a brief visit to the loo, only to find on their return it has been tidied away (probably in a place where it can't be found). Even stringent safeguards never entirely work, and in order to help us in the right direction my own community occasionally mutters a semi-humorous motto: "never be helpful". I suppose, strictly speaking, the problem is not about helpfulness but awareness; and then it's about realism too. It pays to check the real facts before taking charge, but it pays as well to be realistic about the need for any action in the first place. Will serious consequences follow with the dustpan left where it is, or might it, to be honest, just as well stay there? Is there a sufficient possibility of intruders or draught (or in some cases smell) if the door stands open, or will the world still carry on if you leave it? Any backseat driving has to be executed with this kind of care.

Who's in charge?

Awareness and realism are fundamental in our relationship with God. In our prayer and worship, who is in charge? In less managerial terms, how far is it realistic for me/us to assume we are the active ones, both in private prayer and in public worship? Obviously, in worship, if we don't do anything nothing will happen; we do need to act in some way. But worship demands of us quite a bit of finesse if we are not to end up as backseat drivers. One helpful image is the knob that controls the balance between two loudspeakers. Where on the calibrated circle is our level of contribution, and where is God's level on it? In the history of the Church, and more today than perhaps at any other time in Christian history, our worship is often dominated by backseat driving. Poor old God is meant to meet the requirements and expectations we identify and set, and to relate to us in the schemes we devise. It is not straightforward. An act of worship can be fully planned with a teaching aim in mind, and with little waiting upon God. Another may be prepared with great reverence, and yet be utterly unaware of the degree to which it is human-centred. The way we lead worship is particularly prey to these pitfalls. In the older Catholic tradition, the priest always had to look down and never engage the eyes of the people—this seems to fail in the opposite direction, for God is encountered in human engagement too. In monastic life, there is less scope for human-centredness in worship and prayer—it has to creep in in more veiled ways because of the setup. It can be found in the way the Eucharist is presided over, or the way the singing is led, or in the hopes and aspirations of the brother who has arranged the flowers, or the organist. The prima donna in all of us always looks for its opportunity. But these rather pathetic self-absorptions are peanuts in the midst of the huge rock of daily monastic liturgy, with the meanest of scope for taking too much charge.

This should not be confused with what is going on in the monastic underground. In all worship in religious communities and parishes, sin is busy in many hearts, in temptations, misplaced desires, grudges, self-preoccupation, wandering minds and so on. Monks and nuns and religious brothers and sisters belong with everyone else in this underground, but this question of what is going on in the heart, fascinating as it is, is a different subject, perhaps for another time. What we are exploring here is the overground: how the worship is put on and what goes into it. There is no clear border between that and the inner workings of the heart—they smudge into each other—but we are interested here in who it is that is at the steering-wheel of the outward worship. The monumental rock of the daily liturgy is fine for religious brothers and sisters who have a special calling for working at the divine coalface, mining the inexhaustible seam of the divine love and its truth-revealing searchlights. Worship can't work quite in the same way in a parish, where for most of the time the community is dispersed, and there is not such a sense of the holy mountain of the liturgy and the life. How it works in the parish situation needs a little more careful exploration. Our quest is to sense how in any Christian community the speakers-control is set: in other words, how determining is the human contribution and how determining is the contribution that comes from God?

Once when I was on holiday, I went on the Sunday morning to the local Church of England parish church. In the absence of a priest, the worship was led by members of the congregation. The good folk who had been given the responsibility had prepared a service all about local life—the village, work on the land, the community's experiences and needs. There was no mention of the universal Church, no intimation that we were part of a great mysterious reality greater than us, the Body of Christ. The service was entirely worthy and sincerely meant, but through no fault of their own the folk responsible had not been adequately equipped to prepare the main public service on a Sunday in a parish church. There were sensitive human insights, expression of good human aims, and a sense of one group deciding from its own resources what would be good to do, but I came away feeling I had been invited, feeling slightly mystified and extraneous, into a group and its world, rather than the Body of Christ.

Creative worship

Worship which follows its own path, devised by one person or team from scratch, plays quite a large part in Christian life today. Typical might be the grouping of everyone around a candle with perhaps some other visual aids, and then, say, the taking of a stone or pebble, reflecting on it, then one by one putting it in a significant place. There will be a message given in thoughts and prayers, in an atmosphere of concentration and devotion. In training institutions of the churches of the Reformation in particular, this kind of worship can loom large. Certainly, the ordained need to be trained to use their imaginations, not least in pastoral circumstances where something tailor-made is needed, or worship with children, or acts of prayer expressing the life of particular groups; and imagination and inventiveness have their part to play in any act of worship, whatever its nature. But there is a problem when what I have described supplants the life-giving breathing in and out of the day-to-day liturgy. I hope to show why this kind of homemade worship, and private prayer, while having its place, needs to take particular care that it is not human-resourced backseat driving. One force behind a lot of worship today is a desire to make it attractive, to make it have an effect on people, an effect that will make them feel good, and might attract people who aren't inclined to go to church.

Many years ago, in a weekly column in *The Times*, Bernard Levin castigated church people who were trying gimmicks, as he saw it, to attract people to church, and said something like, "If only they would realize that if people saw someone totally engrossed with looking towards the sun, they would want to tiptoe up behind them and look over their shoulders to see what was holding their attention." It may be that one of the things mission needs to concentrate on is attention. In religious communities it is partly a silent, interior attention, but also the attention of our bodies. It is holistic, as much present in the daily singing and reciting as in the Eucharist, and in the practices of the refectory, and the way meetings are held, the way the work is done, and the way visitors are received and people are ministered to. It is not just mental. How may this attention to the sun be expanded in our parishes into practices that bring the whole person, body and soul, as community, into a "wondrous trafficking" (*admirabile commercium*) with God, as a Christmas antiphon puts it, without the need for such heavy-handed engineering of outcomes on our part?

Our picture of God

Behind what I have called backseat driving lurks an insidious temptation—the temptation to believe in our picture of God. An act of worship can conjure up the picture of God we want—or at least the one we have. Every person, believing or non-believing, has presuppositions about God, mental pictures: they will always be short of the mark, always something of a caricature. If you are asked to imagine daily life in Ulan Bator, and then win a weekend ticket for a holiday there, you will quickly realize, as you explore the town and meet the people, how hopeless your imagined picture was. Hopefully with God we have received a little more input and will not find ourselves so completely wrong-footed. Our mental pictures will be pretty wide of the mark, nonetheless. We have to put aside our picture of God—never trust it. When people struggle with prayer or find it difficult, the root cause can be just this: our picture of God. This is true for everyone, including members of religious communities. When I spend time in prayer, I try and set aside my involuntary mental imagining of God, as it always distorts. In worship, the danger always lurks, and is never completely avoided, of setting up a humanly contrived mask we aim the worship at, rather than the actual Lord who asks us to seek more gingerly. In Psalm 115, we are warned against false gods and idols:

They have mouths, but they cannot speak;
eyes have they, but they cannot see;
They have ears, but they cannot hear;
noses, but they cannot smell . . . (vv. 5–6).

Jesus doesn't tell us anywhere that we can see God in our head. The disciples ask to see the Father, and in John's Gospel, Jesus is reported as saying ,"Whoever has seen me has seen the Father" (John 14:9). Where we do see and touch, hear and taste is in the scriptures and the sacraments, in the Church, and in the Church's repertoire of practices. Because of their sacramental nature Christ is to be encountered in them, and we get inklings of the God who we cannot see either with our eyes or in our imaginings. This precedes any pictures in our head and enables us to know that God is closer to us than we are to ourselves, Christ in us, the hope of glory. We just need to be careful of our picturing.

One picture of God which is popular today is a view that God is exciting. Now of course, what could be more exciting? I think immediately of a hymn sung at Mattins in Advent: "O hear the voice whose thrilling song bids shadows of the night be gone . . .". For the hymn's ninth-century author, Christ's thrilling and exciting voice fills us with hope. Of course, "exciting" is one of the words we can't help using as Christians, but it does feel overused today if we consider that God is also daunting, challenging, oblique in his workings, can make us angry, can withhold what we want. A wide range of sentiments comes into play in traditional liturgy: praise and thanksgiving, wonder and delight, but also petition, penitence, lament, questioning, struggle and requests for mercy. More widely, a frequent compliment people make about a service or a project is that it is exciting. It is less common for us to praise an act of worship for its seriousness. The well-known icon of the Trinity by Rublev shows the three visitors to Abraham by the oak at Mamre: these visitors turn out to have been a visitation from God, and it has been natural to associate these visitors with the Trinity. People say of the faces in Rublev's icon that they are quietly joyful faces. Contrastingly, it is also often said they are sad or lamenting or, perhaps better, profoundly serious faces. They manage to be both. Christian celebration, unlike the world's celebration, embraces seriousness and lament as well as joy. Rowan Williams has said somewhere that too often representations of the resurrection are merely triumphant, but the resurrection embraces everything: the light and the dark of life, the wonderful and the awful. On the Resurrection altar in our church at Mirfield, there is a carving by Nicholas Mynheer of the risen Jesus breaking bread with the two disciples in the inn at Emmaus. We asked him to give a sense in his sculpture that everybody is there, all of humanity in the background, with all their joys and their sorrows. The cross and the resurrection are one thing. Our secular society will puzzle at how it is possible to celebrate something as dark as the Cross, but for Christians Christ's cross, and the following resurrection, is a powerful generator of wonder and celebration, as well as sorrow, seriousness and longing.

Worship is received

One cardinal principle is that worship is closest to what God desires when in its essentials it is *received*, not created on the spot. You may object that everything in worship was in its time created on the spot, but there is a point here about the passage of time. With the years the original authors recede into the background, and what is lasting has been sifted, while also gaining depth and associations of its own not foreseen in the original creation. The liturgy, and much of Christian prayer, comes from elsewhere, not from us here. David Brown has reflected on this and shown that words are often at their most powerful when they cease to be closely aligned with the original intentions of their authors.[31] Worship created on the spot has its place, of course, but not in prime time on a Sunday, unless part of a journey towards the liturgy and the sacraments, as family services or, say, Messy Church are (ideally) intended to be. Elements created on the spot may be particularly necessary in something like a difficult funeral, or a one-off special occasion, but that should not be confused with the true on-the-spot contribution found in how an act of worship is celebrated well, and how we pray and participate, things

---

[31]   David Brown, *God and Enchantment of Place* (Oxford: Oxford University Press, 2004), p. 161.

that make the difference between it feeling alive or dead. Again we come to our loudspeakers' control knob: getting the right balance between the two sources. Everything has its place, but "creativity" ought not to be enthroned, giving the true Creator and Lifegiver little room for the royal way in worship, always more mysterious and oblique than we can readily handle.

If a service is to be the prime act of worship on a Sunday it needs (a) to reflect a commonality with the way Christians are praying all over the world, and a sense of their presence with us and ours with them—in other words, a strong sense of the Church; and (b) to draw strongly on the repertoire of Christian practices, especially those that are shared by all and nourished from the depths of history, with more of a genetic sense of Christianity's "language". Our creativity cannot simply have free rein: it has to have due regard, and to be well informed. People need proper training.

The rock of the liturgy

Prayer needs toughness. In the monastic life, we have said that it is like a huge rock that is non-negotiable. You don't take shortcuts or give in to moods. You do it, every day, come hell or high water, even if it seems empty or appears not to meet our needs. In the Roman Catholic Church of the Middle Ages, this developed into language of "obligation", a legal requirement. In many walks of life, however, there is a better way of looking at such a call upon us, as it is in marriage, where any sense of what the individual legally owes is overtaken and left behind by a living and loving (if not always easy) bond, where you simply know that this is who you both are. This sense of the rock of the liturgy and of prayer is difficult to find the right images for, and is no monopoly of monasteries—it is what Christ calls us to. Prayer, with the Church, in the Tradition, is simply there, like a mountain or the sea, and this is who we are.

Since the start of the Covid-19 lockdown, my community has live-streamed all its services every day. One comment we receive is of the effect on people as they see an unstinting offering of worship five times a day, impressing on them a sense of something solid and orientating. Others speak of encountering a powerful experience of Christian orthodoxy, coming as they often do from a life full of relativism and the wishy-washy. For the community members, the rock-like Daily Prayer has an absolute call upon us, and everything just needs to fit around it. Once one of our brethren genuflected, fell over and died just before Evensong. While one went to call the doctor, the sacristan threw a glorious cope over the brother, and Evensong went ahead as normal, in his presence. Once when I was a novice, the Chapter was having crisis discussions about a situation in another country where a brother had become a figure in a civil war that was going on, and it was not easy to know what to decide. There were soldiers on the streets around the priory where the brother was, and the country's prime minister's office wanted a response from our meeting. To my astonishment, at a certain point a bell rang and the community simply abandoned the discussion to go to church for the midday office, and the discussion could only be resumed later on. As St Benedict says, nothing must be put before the *Work of God*, as he called the liturgy. It might look outlandish, but it doesn't once you have got under the skin of this understanding of prayer, where to fail in our covenanted turning to God is not normally on the cards.

We do it because we do it

There is a temptation to treat the gospel as a programme for human living, to be put into effect by human efforts, perhaps with helpful backup from "spirituality". The subtle reaches of this might not be noticed, but such an approach, worthy as it may be, would nosedive pretty quickly in a religious community. This is because the poverty of humanity acting on its own, out of its own human resources, is quickly exposed by the life. You are exposed to yourself, and there is no running away. Solitude, silence, a disciplined routine, and being eyeball-to-eyeball with a group of people you haven't chosen, simply exposes the poverty of our human resources and our dependence on God. This dependence is lived out personally and physically. On the subject we are discussing, the physical practicality of Daily Prayer is simply there like breathing. You feel like not getting out of bed, but you get up and do it. You are in the middle of an important task which you can't leave, but you leave it nonetheless, and go and do it. You feel blank, grumpy, worn out, but you go and do it. You are on holiday, feet up at last, but the time comes round and you do it. Religious communities are lucky to have a setup that is monumental, and in addition everyone is watching. The Venerable Bede said he could not miss Mattins because the angels would say, "But where is Bede?" That is even before Bede reckoned on the other brothers thinking the same thing.

It is a challenge to see how far this demanding discipline is relevant to Christians as a whole. Monks and nuns are what they are—for everyone else life is different. We can say, first of all, however, that something comparable is applicable to ordained clergy. Through most of history some discipline of this kind has been assumed to go with the job, if you are commissioned as the Lord's representative. From the Middle Ages, it came to be spoken of in a language of obligation, but the Church can't have a healthy spiritual life if it depends on being policed. In their initial formation, the clergy need to make a journey of discovery in which they come to see the point (the penny drops). The hump to be passed over here is about seeing prayer and the pursuit of holiness as absolute in the life of Christians, like looking after a baby, or running a farm. You can't skip it when you feel like it. This is our gold standard.

When it comes to the Christian people as a whole, having a sense of obligation was something that used to work in some settings, but can do so no longer. Rather than rules or obligations, Christ encouraged his followers to take responsibility, and didn't micro-manage. Baptism means taking responsibility and having a sense of responsibility for the Church's life and mission. In Chapter 6, in the section about the parish's prayer, I suggested a network approach, and this might help foster a sense of holding responsibility, moving away from top-down structures. We all need encouragement too. St Benedict in his Rule says that when the brethren get up in the morning, they should encourage each other in the midst of their sleepiness. Christian maturity can lead us to the point that God reached in the creation of the world. God looked at it and saw that it was *good*. We can discover that good for ourselves in worship and prayer, a good to be pursued for its own self, and out of it, miracles happen. In my own community, you have a group of bachelors who ought, by all accounts, to be pretty irritated with each other and wanting to escape, whereas in fact, even though sometimes we may grind our teeth, we love one another, find joy and mutual enlargement in one another, and find we are growing and changing all the time. Other miracles follow—people helped; people encouraged; insights gained and shared; folk wanting to come for more. Our life of prayer needs to be sufficiently strong for us to reckon we are not simply acting out of our poor and limited human resources and vision, but are being expanded and guided.

We have reached a point where it would be good to look at some examples of Christian worship, assessing them in the light of the criteria we have established, especially the Church, Tradition, Eucharist and Daily Prayer.

St Mega's

We begin with an imaginary parish, full of energy and attracting large numbers. We can call it St Mega's. The worship here is led by a music group at the front, one of whom may play a leading role in guiding the worship. The soft-rock music is performed with professionalism and the singing is rousing, energizing the congregation in a powerful experience. There is a sermon at some point by an ordained minister, and then a time of prayer and reflection often led by someone else, ending in some more praise. The words of the songs, it is often said, are not strong on content; there is an emphasis on personal faith in Jesus, and people's appreciation of the worship tends to use the criterion of whether one can feel it has been "good worship". A "sense of the Church" as we have been discussing it is not greatly in evidence—the emphasis is on this experience now, and on the personal faith of each individual; the service depends very much on "experience"—particularly on having a good one.

One question we have to ask is what the best place is for worship of this kind—not whether it is good or bad, which anyway is a difficult question to tackle about any worship. The worship at St Mega's is one of the things Christians do, so what is its proper place in Christian life? It can, for instance, be effective in introducing the gospel to people in our society. It is one way of doing mission—honey, if you like, to draw into the Christian community those who can respond to this particular type of worship and music. It also responds to the desire of some already-committed Christians for worship in this style. Our key question concerns worship on the Lord's Day and the festivals of the Christian year and, following closely on that, Daily Prayer. According to our four signposts of Church, Tradition, Eucharist and Daily Prayer, we have to say that this worship does not impart a strong sense of the Church universal, or of doing what the Church does, partly because it is not the Eucharist and therefore does not regard itself as sitting within and drawing upon the great Christian Tradition. We need not doubt that the Christians taking part pray every day, and that the service arises out of a context of Daily Prayer, but we have to ask whether that Daily Prayer itself follows our four criteria—is it the prayer of the People of God or is it individual-centred or group-centred? In addition, we need to ask questions about expressions of "personal" faith—certainly important for all of us, but where is it being positioned on the ladder? Is it being *enthroned*, when its proper place should be shoulder-by-shoulder with other things?

One additional problem is that the Church's liturgy is a treasure-house of well-considered and tested theology and understandings of the Christian calling, whereas much of the content of these services is in songs whose theological content cannot rise to such a high standard (one thinks, for example, of the prevalence of penal substitution theories of the atonement), and yet the worshippers only have *this* to shape and inform their faith. There seems little reason why the Sunday worship should not be the Eucharist—but if it is to be, then how might that work? Are there communities that worship in this way but centre it on the Eucharist?

An African experience

To explore that a little further, we now go to Africa, to a large church with a roof and no walls, and tiered seating for large numbers. Hundreds of people are energetically singing and dancing in a service that lasts for four hours or so. These good folk are really enjoying themselves—all ages, young and old, and plenty of children. Life is no doubt tough in varying degrees, but they have the gift people in many parts of Africa are uniquely blessed with, an unselfconscious instinct to dance and sing and enjoy the wide range of possibilities the human body offers for movement and expression, with sheer joy. They like being together, and they love this music and this worship. The charismatic movement has played a big part in liberating people in Africa to be their dancing selves in worship, and here it is in full swing. About halfway through, the music stops and the Eucharist is celebrated. It is done with dignity, and even with incense and a Gospel procession. Then when it is over the music and dance resume for another couple of hours. I was impressed, and if I raise a question about it, this may well be a misreading by a mere outsider. My question was about whether the Eucharist had not simply been an interlude that had to be done, but was not integrated very much with what came before and after. Could it not, I asked myself, rather become a four-hour Eucharist that gave Eucharistic shape and purpose to the whole service, while integrating within itself this style so natural to people, and such a breath of fresh air for them in the midst of their daily lives? There were here two gifts which, if integrated, would move the whole thing onto another level. It would not be enough to alter the design of the service—a door would need to be opened up for people that would lead to greater desire to engage with the Eucharist itself. St John's Gospel shows Jesus going to great pains to teach the disciples about the bread of life. St Paul, however, had to give supplementary teaching to the Corinthians (see 1 Corinthians 11), because they were not grasping its full significance. Our life in the Eucharist needs to be backed up all the time by sustained reflection—it does not always reveal its secrets automatically. It needs to be thought about as well as celebrated. If we think of the degree to which Christians at the moment think hard about mission and about service of our neighbour, we get a picture of the degree to which energies need to go into thinking about the Eucharist.

A German experience

Grateful for our African experience, however, we now go to Germany. Ralf is a Roman Catholic parish priest in the ancient town of Trier (in German there is no equivalent to "Father" for addressing priests). Some of the congregation in this traditional Gothic church were open to change, and at a certain point the seats were experimentally rearranged into rows facing each other college-wise, and a small nave altar set up. Social events brought people to know each other better, and then came the launch of what developed into a perpetual round-the-year event called "sredna", the German word for "differently" written backwards. The principle was worship within the Tradition, with people being themselves and relating together. Special events, performances, imaginative worship at the different festivals and traditions of the year, all revolve around the Eucharist every Sunday. Quite soon a great variety of people were coming through the door for events which could be spiritual, cultural or artistic—most visitors just passing through, but the congregation itself gently growing. You might call the worship "happy-clappy", but happy-clappy with teeth: people are discovering how to be more themselves in church through becoming an avowedly accepting community. In the congregation is a group of deaf people. A special moment for Ralf was after the Easter Vigil one year, when this group joined in a dance on the street outside the church. He said they were instinctively afraid to dance for fear of making a mess of it through not hearing the music, but now felt sufficiently at home to let themselves go, in an unexpected and special moment.

Ralf insists that something important for the parish is staying with the Tradition. That means the Eucharist is at the heart of the parish's worship, and for it to be so, a lot of imagination and self-giving is needed—self-giving in the sense of being the real human beings that we are in the midst of the twenty-first-century world. Not rattling off forms of words without imagination, not being content that certain things are merely done, not being satisfied with avoidance and distance in relationships. Ralf often arranges special forms of vespers and other traditional services, enabling them to become part of adults' and children's lived Christian experience, and the congregation makes the most of the seasons of the year and special local traditions on saints' days. Parents wanted a regular family service for their children, and Ralf said it would be a Eucharist. They said, "We don't want that—it's formal and boring—lots of words from the priest." He said, "We won't do it like that." The way he did do it they liked, and it has stuck.

Some people in the parish asked to study the Eucharist, saying what they were taught as children no longer worked. From those classes, ideas evolved on how to teach the children. This led to First Communion classes in the parish, which fulfil a similar role to confirmation classes in Anglicanism. Each one is a big event, with large numbers of youngsters, and parents with clear ideas about how they think everything should be done, because it has always been done like that, even if they themselves do not go to church very often. Now it has all changed, starting with a party, stories and happy-clappy singing. He tells them at the end, "If you're interested, come again next week." There are just four meetings in the church, not more. At the first, they act out the origins, using not the Gospels but 1 Corinthians. They learn about the people in this port city. There was secrecy about it—children act out knocking on the door and giving a password and so on. After the first time of doing this, Ralf said, "This opens a really new way of thinking, including for myself. The Corinthians had never met Jesus, they were founded by a guy who hadn't seen Jesus. This was the children's own situation." The Corinthians were learning by their mistakes to live with a fundamental equality between all people—Greeks and Jews, poor and rich, and all the others—and they were one body. Jesus had said to his disciples, "I'm dying now—you are now this body—this bread is what it is about." In one class, the children broke a loaf and then tried to see if they could put it back together again but couldn't. But this bread can do it—in us. Ralf took some large priest's hosts and broke them into smaller pieces and gave each child a piece to take home, as a sign that we are one body. Some parents took it and ate it; one father said, "No, that's wrong, that's not for us—take it back," and the little boy brought it back the next week, learning thereby something of the difficulty of sharing the message even with those you love.

After they have made their First Communion, they return as it were to Corinth. A long table is set up the length of the nave, bearing doughnuts, chocolates, cakes and orange juice. At its West End stand cross and Bible, and at the other the small square nave altar bearing the Eucharistic gifts, purposely slightly higher than the table—the connection is clear, but there is no confusion between tables. In the side aisles are tables at which children can write their evaluations and reflections. The party climaxes with the Eucharist celebrated at the altar.

There are three stages in the course: Participate, Understand, Love. Some children drop out as they encounter each, but plenty stay on right through and engage with enthusiasm. On the parish website, accompanying material is posted, explaining what is done at each stage. One parent looked Ralf earnestly in the eye at the end of the course and said, "What you want is a revolution. Well—I'm on board."

Amongst the adults, Ralf says, there is now a sense of ownership and a joy at being there, and people know each other better. Here perhaps is a sign of one way in which the Tradition can be carried forward to the benefit of all. Awareness can grow through learning about the historical development of worship. If we are looking for an example of Christians being unskilled, we should reflect that we can go to church for years, and repeatedly do things without knowing why we do them and why these things are there. There needs to be more teaching about worship, and more competent formation of clergy for the task. The Church needs to be a Berlitz language school of its own language, its tradition. Every Christian is capable of well-informed liturgical competence—there is no reason why that should be beyond the abilities of any Christian congregation, guided professionally by their clergy. Christians deserve to be taught about the liturgy by people who have gained the competence to do so.

Sredna is run by a large team of lay people, and Ralf sees it as the glue that holds everything together. The experience at the Sacred Heart Church in Trier gives a good example of a contemporary approach to living the Tradition and the Eucharist that attracts young people and the unchurched and has porous borders, drawing in further people who are not practising Christians, while also making an unusual contribution to the ordinary life of the locality. That kind of worship is not for everybody, but the Church today needs to be a network of unified diversity (see Appendix).

St Gregory's San Francisco

Our next example is St Gregory's Episcopalian Church in San Francisco. When you walk into their worship, you might initially think you were in an Eastern Orthodox church, then quickly realize this is something else. There are colourful sacred ministers galore, with lavish use of church traditions, chants and artefacts, but a carefully thought out theology undergirds this apparent serendipity, strongly reliant on Gregory of Nyssa and the Cappadocian Fathers. Finding a way to describe in mere words the worship at St Gregory's is a challenge, and a more accurate impression can be gained from videos on their website.[32] When you enter, you find yourself in a colourful octagon, with the altar table at its centre. The walls around are decorated with frescoes of saints ancient and modern in a Byzantine style. Beyond the octagon is a long space with an apse: this is the seating area, and at its further end is the presider's chair. The congregation is far from sedentary, however: this building is an open arena for a drama in which all present are actors, much as was true of the early Christian basilicas. Near the seating area stands a lectern platform bearing a large menorah, lamps and incense. There is a large group of ministers, priests, deacons and others, but further adults and children and first-time visitors are recruited just before the service starts, to ring bells and gongs, light lamps and candles, and prepare incense and other items. Everyone gathers in the octagon.

As the procession enters, bells stop ringing and the cantor leads a choir chant; the ministers kiss the altar and then go round the congregation greeting people. When the music stops, a gong is rung and the presider greets everybody: "Christ is risen!—*He is risen indeed!*" The cantor announces the number of the next chant, and all sing as the whole assembly processes to the seating area. Then a blessing and the Incense Hymn. After another chant all sit for the reading, and after more singing, the Gospel is read. For the participatory sermon, the preacher sits in the middle, and anyone raising their hand is invited to illustrate with a personal story what they are hearing. Then in the Gospel procession, all have the opportunity to reverence the Gospel book. A deacon leads a

---

[32] <https://www.saintgregorys.org/videos.html>, accessed 17 October 2023.

litany with sung responses, and then ministers and congregation move to the altar area, everyone dancing together in a simple dance movement, based on the ancient *tripudium* step. Once gathered around the altar, the Peace is shared. After the Eucharistic Prayer and breaking of the bread, Communion is taken among the crowd—it is offered to all, baptized or not, on the reckoning that Christ broke down barriers rather than putting them up. Afterwards the Cantor announces: "*We'll sing and dance the carol . . . Carols are sung dances, and we'll make it easy for you to dance the carol by surrounding you with people who've done it before. The step is simple. Starting on your right foot—step to the right and slide your left foot together, step to the left and slide your right foot together. Step to the right, feet together—step to the left, feet together. Step to the right, feet together—step to the left, feet together.*" At the end of that, a deacon sings, "Let us bless the Lord!—*Thanks be to God!*"

This worship is unexpected and original, while rooted strongly in the repertoire of the Tradition. The music is nothing like the hymn-singing we are used to, nor the worship songs widespread today. It is classical, demanding, and yet singable by anyone of any age. The worship is undergirded by liturgical and theological scholarship. Furthermore, it revels in an Aladdin's cave of items and practices and engagement of the body. It is very San Francisco: extrovert, multicultural, confident. It has inspired people in many countries, and it also makes some very angry. Whatever your response, however, it is difficult to deny that all will have things to learn from it.

Tradition of our time

We can see from these examples that it is possible to worship in the Tradition in a way that reflects our contemporary culture. This kind of worship is far from the quiet and mysterious atmosphere of monasteries, but it shares the same foundations, and encompasses a different range of things from the present sterile contrast between "traditional" and "contemporary" worship, as they are commonly thought of. They illustrate the theme of "practices" that we are exploring through this book: the Church, the Tradition, and the Eucharist as the cornerstone of Christian worship, especially on Sundays, building on the Tradition to evolve and expand the repertoire of Christian practices. Such practices help to put backseat driving, or human-centred assumptions and attitudes, less in the foreground.

Worship as work

The question of who in fact is doing the driving will never cease to exercise the antennae of anyone who cares about it, for we still have to ask it; we are human beings, and sin is bound to be at work in some way in all of this. Have we yet done enough to make ourselves aware of how far God is in the driving seat, and how far we can be backseat driving? The monastic tradition maintains what you could call a serene wariness. St Benedict's term for worship, "God's work", is two-pronged. It states that all worship is God at work. We are carried to God by God, and not anybody else. Secondly, Benedict's Latin, *Opus Dei*, can be taken to mean that worship is work, not entertainment, or stirring up of approved feelings, or even necessarily pleasure or "uplift" or stirring the heart, or having a religious experience. It is something you simply get on with whatever you might feel about or be "getting out of" it. Just as building and sustaining a family and its relationships needs a lot of work, effort, sacrifice of self, so too with worship: it needs work in every participant. Sometimes we may experience good or helpful things, but there are times when we won't, and that is OK. I am not always likely to judge well what God is doing for me and others in worship, while my deep, unconscious being is always affected without my knowing.

Getting something out of it

The powerful influence of our society can give us an expectation that worship and private prayer should give us an immediate experience. Life itself gives us something else, however. Take family life—if we carried into family life the expectations of good experience that we bring to worship, we would quickly be brought to a halt. If you look at family life, you find it full of liturgies, often without any visible emotion. We would drive each other mad if we were wanting a feel-good experience all the time out of each other. Life is not like that. Often we go about things fairly vaguely, but all the time there is stuff going on beneath the surface, not at the top level of our immediate experience but in our deeper layers. These may all then well up, for instance, at the time of a family tragedy.

It is often said of Christian liturgy that you just get on and do it in just this sort of way. Sometimes you may be able to say you have had a good experience, or you have felt you have worshipped; but you can't expect that all the time, for if you expect a good experience, then there is a great temptation to engineer it, by always laying on exciting music, for instance. The living tradition of the liturgy, which is just like the tradition of the English language, is changing our spiritual atoms and molecules belowdecks. Think of a furniture maker, a craftsman or craftswoman. They spend years making beautiful furniture without having great revelations or experiences when they are doing it, but after many years you find this person has developed an expert judgement about the craft. The development of a sense of judgement is a good illustration of how the liturgy works with us. You do it faithfully and lovingly, and often perhaps without seeming to get a lot out of it, but you trust it—you know that it is laying down in you slowly a sense of judgement—or in this case an ever-more rooted being-with-God. Another helpful image is sedimentation. The Christian pilgrimage with God in prayer and worship and service of our neighbour is often unremarkable, but a constant sedimentation is going on in us of divine things.

Courtship and covenant

If this is the case, why bother with special effects? Why not do without music and art and other practices, and keep it simple? Why not make it pure work? Some religious traditions have attempted that, but it is not at all obvious that the fruits of such abstinence are beneficial. It can be helpful here to identify two modes in worship: wooing and covenant, parallel in their way to courtship and marriage. Wooing seeks to gain the head and the heart, the whole human being, in drawing people to Christ.

In a mission in a parish, for instance, the acts of worship may be fairly informal, in a popular vein, with an aim to encourage in the participants a willingness to go further. Ralf's First Communion classes are strongly wooing. It is here that some aspects of the free worship I have described come into their own. The aim and hope is that some people at least will be so attracted that they will go forward to a more mature commitment to or covenant with God. Once you have covenanted and committed yourself, however, just as in marriage, or in a job, you get on with it without looking for feel-good moments all the time.

Both these two modes, wooing and covenant, are always there in the committed Christian life. Although worship is work, and the really committed person will simply get on with it, whether it moves them or not, there always needs to be some element of "wooing", elements that will touch the heart and the feelings, encouraging and firing up each Christian and community in the work of worship. Even in monastic life this is the case: one community of Trappist sisters in Italy sings all the offices in beautiful harmony—they say that their life and worship are generally so austere that they need to have some point where the heart is not neglected. If worship veers too much, however, to the side of wooing, or goes all for it, for a good experience that will make everyone feel great, the deeper fruits of the covenant life are likely to be lost; even more, something is put out of court between God and us. When we are planning worship, preparing its music, laying out the place where it is to be held, there is always going to be an inclination towards getting what we want, through getting the worship to do what we want it to do. We might be wanting to project our picture of God (always, as we have seen, a dodgy enterprise), or bring about for the participants what we (and perhaps they) think they need. God, meanwhile, has other things in store which we can't foresee and will miss if we are not careful. The situation will never be perfect, but it is at least good to be aware of the pitfalls, aware of the drawbacks of too much concentration on worship's effects and "feel".

Stirring the heart in parish and monastery

The monastic tradition is interesting here. In parish worship, efforts are usually made to engage the heart through the choice of music and words and visual presentation, and through warm expression of community. As a child I grew up in a parish where the main Sunday worship was "High Mass"—the ministers dressed in splendid vestments, there was an abundance of servers and candles and incense and bells, and often processions and special practices. As a child, I took it for granted, but later as a teenager I came to be thrilled by it. The effect of splendid ceremonies performed by the parish in which all felt they were involved together was a powerful thing which has never left me. Formal ceremonies, beautiful vestments and all the rest have an ability to stir the heart and convey a sense of the grandeur and mystery of what we are about. They also reveal the great dignity of what it is to be human beings, when the ministers are dressed like royalty. It powerfully evokes a sense of the Church as a mysterious entity bigger than us. There is something happening here which we can find also in military ceremonies—the formality and the stirring dress give you a sense of belonging to something bigger than you, that is greater than you, and a source of a life greater than you, and stirs you, sounding your deeps.

In monastic life, by contrast, there is a long tradition of shunning such things, not out of rejection, but for another reason, which could be put like this: in a church where beautiful things are done for the glory of God, there needs to be somebody around to remind us of the hidden pitfalls. Some can be so excited by the worship that it upstages God, and some ministers so affected by wearing splendid robes that it unhelpfully boosts their egos. Worship of this kind can elicit group or institutional pride. Institutional pride is something that monastic communities can be particularly prone to, and a strong and repeated strand in monasticism has always been the desire to witness to the other side of the coin. So the services of religious communities can have a great simplicity. Beautiful things and vestments and music are not rejected, but it is as if the volume control on them is turned right down. The vestments may be good but simple, and the music will usually be a simple melodic line (Western monasticism didn't use polyphony or harmony until modern times).

There is nothing very conscious in all of this, but a gentle probing beneath the things that get us excited.

The fourth-century Desert Fathers were notorious for avoiding grand liturgy. St Benedict never mentions it in his Rule. The Cistercian reform of the twelfth century included a rebellion against liturgy that had become too elaborate, undermining the life. So they prescribed just one candlestick on the altar, not made of precious metal; gold chalices were not allowed; chasubles had to be of linen or wool, without decoration, and copes, dalmatics and tunicles were forbidden. An interesting phrase used was "fidelity to the nature of things, rather than to embellishment"—a principle that has applied in much modern art and design ("form follows function" runs the oft-quoted principle). The great Cistercian abbot Aelred of Rievaulx (1110–67), famous for his writings on friendship, said that "external splendours are miserable"—perhaps a little extreme. St Bernard of Clairvaux (1090–1153), the Cistercian co-founder, said that too much charming of the eyes damages poverty, and dulls our interior sensibility. The Bursfeld Congregation reform in Germany in the fifteenth century followed similar principles. A writer on this reform says of Johannes von Rode, its instigator, that "daily worship should not be in a splendour that on some feasts can be really exciting, but leaves behind an inner emptiness". Rode wanted worship in the monastic choir that feeds the life of the monks so simply and naturally that it is like daily bread for the body. These examples show us a concern that the worship should be real—that it should reflect the lives of the worshippers, and not something else, and in religious communities those lives are dedicated to simplicity.

Religious communities have sometimes taken a different road, adopting the secular Church's splendours, and there have been times when this was needed. Nineteenth-century Anglican religious communities sometimes took such an approach to witness to the beauties of the Tradition in the midst of a struggle against the aridity often blighting the worship of their time. They also sought to encourage parishes to improve their worship by setting an example. At the time, this witness was needed in the Anglican context, to support a long struggle for the reform of the church and its relation to God, and for social reform as well. But in more recent years, we have found ourselves recovering the simplicity of worship that is such a strong thread through monastic history, and also discovering that the monastic gift to the life of the Church is not in trying to imitate what parishes and cathedrals should be doing. Monastic worship has such a power to stir the heart anyway that it has less need of external effects. What speaks is not splendid worship, but the Community and its life. Many visitors, when asked what it is that they value most about visiting our community, say it is "the brethren in church".

This contrast between monastic worship and that of parishes and cathedrals is showing us something important. The monastic community seeks to be searingly honest about what is going on in the human heart, and is surrounded with props to enable it to do so. The worst things that happen in the news or in people's lives are brought into the prayers, however unbearable some of it might be. Tell a seasoned nun of something terrible in your life, something not for the squeamish, and she won't even blink. It is all familiar terrain. The monastic search for nothing but the truth will lead in single-mindedness towards simplicity in worship in the same spirit. Religious communities sit under the life-giving Word, and Rowan Williams has said of them that "there needs to be a basic simplicity of structure in building, art and liturgy so that the plain centrality of the Word . . . can be seen to shape the whole community enterprise".[33]

The parish, by contrast, is set in all the variety of the life of every day, seeking to respond positively to a kaleidoscope, and to some extent to provide a kaleidoscope in response. Some religious communities are involved in parishes or other Christian communities, and there the distinction will not be able to be so simple, but on the whole, in monastic and parish worship we have a contrast between a kaleidoscope and a laser beam. Parish worship will tend towards the kaleidoscopic, monastic towards the laser. This is one of the points where monastery and the parish clearly appear as different organs in the one body, each with its function, but each speaking to the other.

---

[33]   Rowan Williams, "Monastic Virtues and Ecumenical Hopes - Archbishop's address at San Gregorio Magno", 12 March 2012, <http://rowanwilliams. archbishopofcanterbury.org/articles.php/2385/monastic-virtues-and-ecumenical-hopes-archbishops-address-at-san-gregorio-magno.html>, accessed 2 February 2024.

The situation of the Church today

It can be easy to make sweeping statements about the state of the Church at the moment, in a situation too complex for us to grasp. Yet we can see things emerging from the examples in this chapter. First of all, how do we deal well with diversity of practice? Anglicanism has reached a point, at least in places like Britain, where expanding diversity is bringing an increasing and damaging incoherence: key messages now diverge so much that if praxis is not a unifying factor and does not present to its members and to the world a committed coherence, the only thing to do might seem to be to give in and make this tolerant diversity your strong point. One of the gifts of Anglicanism is the way it has been able to hold difference together with a light touch and enquiring minds, but if tolerance is to be the message, it is impossible to turn a tolerance that no longer has braces into a level-one message—it will never be gripping. An opera singer has to have a voice that will rise above 100 players in an orchestra, plus sometimes a choir behind them. Such was the early Church in the Roman Empire: what it lived and said was audible and arresting, and practices were key—love of neighbour, the Eucharist, community in communion, Daily Prayer, a sense of the Church. The worship life of the Church needs to have sufficient overall coherence, and to stand out.

Erik Varden has made a similar comment about Roman Catholic religious communities: "How can we form people to forms that are elastic to the point of becoming diffuse?"[34] There are no easy answers to the problem of speaking with a clear voice while holding together a wide diversity. While the Church of Engand is losing things that the imagination can get its teeth into, the Roman Church seems to have that strange invisible effect of taking the wind out of the sails of many who might be imaginative (except for some spots like the Sacred Heart parish in Trier). Between these pitfalls there will be a way, waiting to be discovered.

---

[34] *The Tablet*, 5 February 2022, p. 13.

Summary

This chapter has explored the idea of putting some trust in the inherited practices of Christianity; it has also explored ways in which Christianity's practices in any age have to engage with the contemporary culture. That exercise always contains dangers, for the culture can easily take over when it should take the role of a servant. One sign of this is when it is expected that worship should "feel good", and in that situation we need to ask searching questions about our picture of God. It requires a balancing act, and it may be that the quest for imaginative worship needs to be tested against the awkward questions raised by monastic simplicity, not in order to imitate it, but to look for what is true.

We can be drawn to God and to what is not-God, all at the same time, pulled, perhaps without realizing it, in two directions. This brings us to a theme that came up earlier in this book: the relationship between living the gospel and living in a society like ours. In many ways, Church and society make two different calls upon us. It would be good here to reflect on how we live both things.

9

Coming into focus

In Chapter 6, we recognized that there is an elephant in the room, which is the obstacles that modern society throws in the way of Christian belief and practice. Many perfectly ordinary and sensible people of our life and time have no problem with being committed Christians. Why, then, do so many other perfectly ordinary and sensible people find it difficult to believe, or even think the whole business irrelevant? In exploring this, we can start with an experience common to all of us.

A motorist suddenly realizes she doesn't know where she has been for the last ten minutes. She has negotiated bends in roads, kept a proper distance from traffic in front, is still on the right route, but has no memory of having done any of this—she was miles away, thinking about other things. A monk who leads the singing suddenly realizes that without a mistake he has been leading complex chants, with their idiosyncratic relationship to the words, while completely caught up in thinking about something else, and he can't remember any of it. No doubt the music could have been sung better and more sensitively, but what is achieved in this absent-minded way can be completely free of mistakes, an experience that can be strange to the point of being creepy. A translator can have the odd experience of simultaneously translating a speaker without either of them pausing—they are simply two people talking at the same time. How is it that we can do two things at once in this way? I am not a neurologist, but one cannot help but think of the dual nature of our brains. The left and right sides, while overlapping to some extent in their operations, have two distinct functions, the left being more analytical, the right grasping the larger integrated picture. However this may be, it is part of human experience sometimes to be living two things at once. The gospel is full of dualities: we are, like the man building the tower, to be prudent in planning for tomorrow, and yet are to take no thought for the morrow; we are to be as wise as serpents and meek as doves; people are condemned for denying parents their due, and yet there is a call to hate our father and our mother. St Paul revelled in paradoxes like the assertion that I am strong through being weak.

Belief and unbelief

One such duality found in Scripture and throughout the Tradition is that between faith and lack of faith, belief and doubt. "Lord, I believe—help my unbelief." Is it possible to believe and not believe at the same time, like driving while thinking about something else? Many of the great saints have written of a sense of the absence of God, which was not itself a crisis of belief; but in our own time, doubt, uncertainty, and struggle with belief are very much part of everyday life. We all know how God is marginalized in our culture, how religious belief is seen as one equal option among many, and the whole climate of our secular world sees no need to take account of God. This climate is invasive; we have grown up in it and are formed by it—it is part of the air we breathe. Human beings are easily affected by the air they breathe and the climate they live in, and it must not be surprising that many Christians struggle with faith today or do not find it in them to live with absolute conviction. For many Christians, the Church is a great help in life, but can be easily given up for one reason or another. In this climate it is important for us to think about how faith sits together with the small voice of unbelief.

I can't but be autobiographical here. For all my Christian life, since being a youngster, I have had the strange experience of sensing I have been taken hold of by God and led, guided, inspired, nudged, rebuked, loved by God, with a strong sense of the divine providence in my life, and a guiding hand; but at the same time a secular wind regularly blows in through the window. This secular wind says something like "God is unbelievable". Often the two go hand in hand. I am mystified by the fact that I feel so at home with God that I seem to have a habitual trust in God's providence, and yet at the same time I can share with my society something at least of its faith vacuum. How is it possible to live these two things at the same time? I must not mislead—this is not about a crisis of faith or a watering-down of it. If anything, it is the reverse. It has taught me one of the main messages of this book. Some forms of Christianity emphasize a "personal faith in Jesus", and I respect what people are trying to say. However, we have to be careful that the language we use is not entirely individual—there is a key part in this, played by the Body of Christ. Christ is not an isolated individual, a lone Palestinian bachelor. One thing I have been forced to learn by the secular wind is the degree to which any understanding of what "faith" means has to be speaking of more than just "me". It has to include the Church as an essential element. Where do I meet Jesus? Certainly in private prayer, to which I shall come shortly. But normally preceding that, and very much so in my case, there is the encounter we have with Jesus in the Body of Christ and its sacramental life and practices. My sights turn to:

- Scripture, poetry, prayers,
- church buildings, font and altar,
- music, beauty,
- icons,
- liturgy, sacraments,
- community,
- love,
- mirrorings of sacrifice and resurrection in loving lives,
- the Church's mystery,
- the gathering-up of the Eucharist,
- profundity of inheritance handed on.

Innately full of the music of all this, I go apart to pray in silence every day. Christ the extraordinary figure of the Gospels holds himself before me who am not an isolated, stumbling solitary, but a person swimming in a symphonic sea. This symphony of people, signs and actions keeps me alert to the abundant life of the gospel. When the secular wind blows in through the window, what follows is not a struggle between it and an exposed, private relationship with Christ, but an encounter with this sea symphony, going down, down into the depths of the water where the wind cannot reach, and the wind finds it is put in its place, remaining frustrated above the surface. What is going on is not a struggle between belief and unbelief—it is something more like a rubbing between the modern mindset and the mystery of the incarnation. This is one of the ways in which members of religious communities are representatives of everybody: we carry within ourselves things that many people in our society carry, and are in a situation where we are brought to train our eyes directly onto them, rather than avoid or hide from them, and to bore down to God who is in the depths—or, rather, to jump aboard God's diving bell. Monastics do this on behalf of everybody, a ministry of empathy, if you like, hand-in-hand with Christ. We all need to be reassured—that we can make our Christian journey even with these contrasting realities sparring within us. The key thing to remember is not to turn it into a battle with the wobbly structure of our own private relationship with God, but rather to turn our eyes to the symphony of signs pouring forth from the incarnation, where we are sensitized to the Christ who is waiting to lead us further. Turn to all the phenomena, people, things, scriptures and actions that make up the rich life of the Church, and let them open our eyes, let them teach us to see.

Struggle with prayer

This windy situation contributes to the struggle many people have with prayer, or their inability to pray, a struggle that includes clergy. Our society keeps up a constant siren song: "this is implausible". Prayer can be like trying to strike a match under water. The not-knowing goes with a misunderstanding that prayer has to be a private effort. Christian prayer can never ultimately be private. People who say they can't pray should be encouraged to look outwards as well as inwards, and to *practise*— to engage in practices of prayer that Christians practise, to make use where they can of church buildings, Christian art and music, to study contemporary Christian thinking, to discover where the church is doing inspiring things, and so on. What might this say about mission? Is a lot of contemporary Christian mission aimed too much at the personal dimension? Perhaps, as I have suggested, we should be offering practical training in Christian practices. An American Jesuit liturgist has given

Luton Parish Church in Hertfordshire as one example of practical mission.[35] The parish church choir, vested in beautiful blue cassocks and full surplices, were shown in a video clip processing and singing through a shopping mall in the town centre, to the pleasure of onlookers, most of whom would not be practising Christians—but there is some scratching here where people itch. Another example would be of a parish which set up scholarships for students to have musical training and sing in the choir. Through this structure of scholarship and singing, non-believing students have discovered the life and worship of the church, and come to a point where they "get it", purely through doing it, swimming in it.

Losing our faith

But what can I say to someone who says they have lost their faith? I would want to say first that the picture they have of God is mistaken, something that is bound to be the case. What they are rejecting is this image. I would tell them to put it aside and delve into the flesh-and-blood reality of the Church that is before their eyes, rather than imaginings in their heads: the people, the worship, reading of the Scriptures, the practices of prayer, the gestures, artefacts, sacraments, church buildings, Christian art and music, the service of our neighbour, the engagement in public life. As a person who cannot believe, give yourself to all of them and see what happens.

Maurice Merleau-Ponty says we need to throw ourselves into the hurly-burly of the physical world. When we are doing something, getting on with a task, not everything is being decided in our head. This becomes particularly clear in a skill like dancing. Our body can know what to do when what is going on in our head does not. We need to throw ourselves into the hurly-burly of the Church, just as the disciples ended up, rather hesitatingly, throwing themselves into the hurly-burly of Jesus' ministry.

Jesus said as much in John 14:8–11:

---

35   John Baldovin, in a public lecture.

> Philip said to Jesus, "Lord, show us the Father, and we will be satisfied." Jesus said to him, "Have I been with you all this time, Philip, and you still do not know me? Whoever has seen me has seen the Father. How can you say, 'Show us the Father'? Do you not believe that I am in the Father and the Father is in me? The words that I say to you I do not speak on my own; but the Father who dwells in me does his works. Believe me that I am in the Father and the Father is in me; but if you do not, then believe me because of the works themselves."

This is an invitation to find belief in Christ's signs.

While many folk show no evident interest in what the Church has to offer, there are those who are genuinely sitting on the threshold. What should they do? Should they try to work out for themselves whether they believe or not? We have already recognized that faith is not first about screwing ourselves up to believe things—it is more about living certain things. Many people who are wrestling with belief might be helped to know that in exploring life with Christ you do not need to shoo away your whisperings of unbelief. Live with both of them and see what happens. Throw yourself into the symphony of signs and its people, and live them. And for those of us who are practising Christians, what if our secular modern world is lurking deep inside us? It is better to meet it head-on than try to cover it up. What will result is not a double life but a single-minded quest for Truth. This duality is on a trajectory towards singleness.

Focus

The oboe gives out a note, the orchestra begin tuning their instruments to fit, sliding up and down until homed in on the same note. This is a theme of the gospel: tuning, focusing, bringing our disparate urges, feelings and desires together into a unity. The word "monastic" derives from the Greek word for "one", firstly in reference to not being married, but single. This singleness goes further, for the monastic is one who seeks singleness of heart. This notion is found throughout the Bible: singleness, purity of heart, the undivided heart. Blessed are the pure in heart, for they shall see God. Our lives are full of preoccupations, tasks, worries and anxieties, struggles, hopes, fears and desires. They pull us in different directions, leaving us with a heart divided, unable fully to reconcile so many things, and feeling to some extent like a juddering engine. Sin has a part to play in it, as we deceive ourselves or others, and as lower urges undermine higher ones. I feel I'll go to help that old person across the road, for instance, but there is another part of me: it does not want to get involved, and that part wins the day. The old person struggles across the road alone. We are not one person but many; we behave differently with different people, in different contexts, and in different moods. We can say one thing while meaning another, tell white lies for the sake of an easy life. "They speak with a double heart" (Psalm 12:2); "purify your hearts, you double-minded" (James 4:8).

The Holy Spirit, if we are willing, will act like a sheepdog, gathering the scattered thoughts and urges, so that gradually all our attention and our energy is directed towards one thing alone, everything pointing in one direction, towards God. However, the sheep is a meek image for what is in us; these things inside us are more like a herd of wild horses that need to be trained to run in the same direction. We repeatedly forget what we are about. This can be particularly glaring in someone who is a publicly marked Christian, such as a priest or a nun or monk. For such a person, to lose their temper with someone who has got in their way on the pavement is a clear instance of momentarily forgetting what we are about. Or we can become so anxious with a task in hand that it can pull us down, and we forget that our life flourishes by being centred all the time on the God who is love, hope and joy. Like a driver, we have to keep our eye on the main road all the time, and have a single eye, trained on one thing. "If your eye is single, the whole body will be full of light" (Matthew 6:22).

John Cassian in the fifth century had some things to say about this. In his *Conferences* he writes:

> The end of our profession is the kingdom of God ... But the immediate aim or goal is purity of heart. For without purity of heart no one can enter that kingdom. We should fix our gaze on this goal and walk towards it in as straight a line as possible. If our

thoughts wander away from it even a little, we should bring our gaze back to it . . . It is for this end—to keep our hearts continually pure—that we do and endure everything . . . If we do not keep this mark continually before our eyes all our travails will be futile waste that wins nothing, and will stir up in us a chaos of ideas instead of single-mindedness.[36]

Simplifying our life

Religious communities have always sought to limit the possibilities for engaging with many things. Simplicity of life takes away some of the possibilities for distraction by limiting the range of things that can have a claim upon us: career, income, possessions, our own home, variety in the wardrobe. But it should not be thought that these restrictions are necessary for every Christian to be able to seek singleness of heart—they are an additional aid for those who are called to it. The Beatitudes were aimed at everybody, and this quest for an undivided heart is for all of us, in whatever walk of life. In a parish community, it points us towards a whole range of ways in which a single heart can be manifest in our lives, much to do with learning to be less centred on self and more loving of others. Of Christ himself, Peter tells us in his first letter:

> To this you have been called, because Christ also suffered for you, leaving you an example, so that you should follow in his steps. 'He committed no sin, and no deceit was found in his mouth.' When he was abused, he did not return abuse; when he suffered, he did not threaten; but he entrusted himself to the one who judges justly. (1 Peter 2:21–3)

If those are signs of Christ's singleness of heart, Colossians spells this out further for us and our own heart:

---

[36]   John Cassian, *Conferences*, Conf. 1, Chapters 4, 5 and 6.

> As God's chosen ones, holy and beloved, clothe yourselves with
> compassion, kindness, humility, meekness, and patience. Bear
> with one another and, if anyone has a complaint against another,
> forgive each other; just as the Lord has forgiven you, so you also
> must forgive. Above all, clothe yourselves with love, which binds
> everything together in perfect harmony. (Colossians 3:12–14)

Singleness of heart, single-mindedness, will issue in an unimpeded,
unqualified love of our neighbour. Either we can be single-minded about
ourselves, selfish, or we can be single-minded about God found in our
neighbour. You cannot have both. It is not easy for any of us to grow
into these generous attitudes of mind, particularly when in most of our
life we are living as the rest of our society lives, a society that is full of
good people, but not all going to the single-minded lengths Christ says
we are capable of.

Being punctured

So for us, ordinary Christians that we are, John Cassian points us towards
something that acts as a door to Christian living, and the name he has for
it is *compunction*. As he explains it, compunction involves a puncturing
or piercing of the heart. It is a moment when Christ pulls us up short
and we are winded. We have a sudden awareness of the sovereign call of
God. It is, if you like, a moment of conversion, although compunction
can seize us many times in our lives. We suddenly see two things: our
own sinfulness and shortcomings, the mess we often make of things, but
also a powerful sensation of the clear and thrilling voice of God, and a
realization that this is a source of life abundant.

Cassian gives four examples of ways in which we can be stirred to
compunction:

1. by the singing of Psalms. Psalm-singing can have the effect of
   stirring the heart and instilling in us a sense of prayer. It is worth
   noting that he cites this very practical activity first;

2. "listening to a spiritual talk by a wise elder"—to which we would add spiritual reading, and all the ways of seeking wisdom that are available to us;

3. news of a death: bereavement inevitably pulls us up short and makes us aware of the transitory nature of life. News of any death of a person we know pulls the carpet from under our feet to some degree;

4. recollection of our own negligence: life's regrets, or embarrassment at recalling actions in the past, are a moment for turning us towards God.[37]

We can see from these examples that compunction can be a thing that comes upon us regularly and in a variety of ways. Rather than being a rare drama, it can prick us at any level of intensity, strong or weak. It is something we can deliberately revisit regularly as part of our prayer.

All manner of things can break through our shell—in my own experience I can think of people affected by the Altar of Repose on Maundy Thursday, or by experiencing an exercise in silent meditative prayer for the first time in their life; someone can be stopped in their tracks by helping with a food bank or some other stark encounter with the tough experiences of others; compunction can come through receiving help with praying (too many Christians struggle without even getting the most elementary help); we can be affected by a visit to a religious community—my own experience of being pulled up short when visiting a bereaved man who clearly needed to hear of God was such a moment of compunction.

Just as the orchestra, as it tunes up, seeks to bring all the disparate tones of its instruments to a point where they sound one single, pure note, so we should find it encouraging to know that even if we sense many things pulling us in different directions, it is possible gradually, over the years, to progress towards singleness of heart. There is even more good news. There is a link between singleness and silence. The less we are pulled in different directions, the more we will find the possibility of an inner stillness. The silence that is part of the climate of a religious community is

---

[37]   John Cassian, *Conferences*, Conf. 9, Chapter 26.

rich, like a symphony. For visitors who come from a hectic, noisy world, this silence can be eloquent and healing. Over recent decades there has been a great rediscovery of this dimension of silence, to such an extent that it is assumed, perhaps too uncritically, that to pray means to go somewhere and be silent. We have to be ready for silence—not everyone is cut out for it straight away, and it can be a mistake to teach Christians that prayer is about being quiet—it can just as well be about being noisy, or at least, as I hope I have shown, about doing things.

The early Christian Fathers say that the Psalms are the prayer of multiplicity, and in the reciting or singing of the Psalms, this prayer of multiplicity gradually leads us to the prayer of simplicity. Some people are naturally given to silence, to being quiet, while others are called to explore the road that begins with multiplicity and leads in a quieter and quieter direction. People can surprise themselves. If a day on prayer is organized in a parish, and at a certain point people are led in an exercise of being silent, some of those there will be amazed at this new and fruitful discovery. Others will not quite be there yet. One great thing about this journey is that unexpected experiences of stillness and singleness can burst in for a short while. Perhaps in a visit to a retreat house or a religious community, or even simply sitting on a beach on holiday. These can be down-payments on the way. Such moments have something to do with the Peace of God which passes all understanding.

Mindfulness and prayer

This leads us to mindfulness—its current popularity is an encouraging sign and can be a step on the way to Christian silent prayer. Mindfulness, however, is largely about being attentive within ourselves, whereas in prayer we are taken further, engaging with a Person outside ourselves, who is also paradoxically at the heart of our being. It is this sense of being taken hold of by Someone which makes prayer more than mindfulness. So it can be helpful to start our prayer with something outside ourselves, such as a story from the Gospels or another part of Scripture, or by looking at an icon. That way we are not starting with ourselves or the things that seem so important to us, when really they are not as important as we think they are. The power they exercise on us needs to be set in a larger space. It is good to start prayer with something which isn't where I am. The silence in the house of a monastery is intended to be the same silence as we find in the chapel; the silence in the corridors, in the refectory, in the public spaces and in our rooms is a form of worship. We are still attending to all that is around us, still listening, still thinking, but human windows are open that otherwise tend to stay shut, and the sound of God's music can drift in.

When people have become settled, pickled in silence, they develop a different attitude to time. If you walk into the sea, your walking gradually gets slower the deeper you get. If you try to run, it is impossible. Even if you start swimming, you will move much slower than walking. And yet the swimming is life-giving, exhilarating, capable of raising gasps of joy. Speed is an overrated criterion. In a religious community, services tend to have plenty of space about them. Prayers can be said slowly and thoughtfully, there may be gaps between the different elements of the service, and a general tendency towards a sense of not being the ones in charge. In my community, we regularly welcome groups, and are used to parish groups rattling through the Lord's Prayer loudly and at a rate of knots, while we have perfected the art, like orchestral players coping with complex modern pieces of music, of holding our own, so that the visitors reach their loud "Amen" only to discover the community just saying slowly and quietly, "give us this day our daily bread". Groups of clergy in particular are notorious for bashing prayers out rapidly and loudly. Worship asks us to listen to one another. In tennis, each player has to operate the racquet at a speed responding to the other—they have to watch each other, watch the ball, and enter into a shared rhythm in order to meet the ball. If a player simply closes their eyes and blindly bashes the racquet backwards and forwards, there will be no tennis. In a worshipping group, we need to listen to each other to speak with one voice, rather than a jumble of different voices each following their own pace regardless. That takes some work and practice—we have to work at it in communities, and there is no reason why such a simple form of practice could not take place in a parish congregation. Mutual listening.

Following on from that, if we are to discover the world of silence, one great help is to look at the pace of our worship, the spaces within it, how people move in the church, and what our assumptions are about who is in charge, who is running this show. God is patient, and happy to wait, but we could just think—a little mindfulness, leading to attention to the One who is in reality in charge, can help on the way. Singleness of heart is not just for individuals: a whole group can grow in it.

Duality, living two things at once, is just one example of the multiplicity of our human nature. If singleness is the goal, we should not imagine that the truth we seek can be neatly boxed up and settled. Truth is always found in a dance that goes on and on, as a multiplicity of things in us gradually, gradually, come together towards a focus.

All for God, all for humans

Austin Farrer in his Bampton lectures gives us another angle on this question of duality, by making a striking comparison between Western poetry and Old Testament prophecy.[38] The prophet Jeremiah cries:

> Cross to the coasts of Cyprus and look,
> send to Kedar and examine with care;
> see if there has ever been such a thing.
> Has a nation changed its gods,
> even though they are no gods?
> But my people have changed their glory
> for something that does not profit.
> Be appalled, O heavens, at this,
> be shocked, be utterly desolate,
> says the Lord,
> for my people have committed two evils:
> they have forsaken me,
> the fountain of living water,
> and dug out cisterns for themselves,
> cracked cisterns
> that can hold no water. (Jeremiah 2:10–13)

---

[38]   Austin Farrer, *The Glass of Vision* (London: Dacre Press, 1948), Chapter VII.

This prophet is no prima donna, no explorer of human feelings: he is giving voice to the sovereign call of God. Farrer says, "We see no evidence of a painful and unconvincing effort to keep the image of God in the centre of the picture. On the contrary, there is a painful effort from time to time to obtrude Jeremiah's private hopes, fears and recalcitrances; but they are forced back, trampled, annihilated by the Word of God."[39] Farrer compares Jeremiah's start-and end-point, of the sovereign voice of God, with Western poetry since the Renaissance, where the starting point is always the human being rather than God, and the poetry always without fail aims to explore what is going on in the human being, and in our response to the world around us. We explore our feelings, ponder our destiny, explore our baseness and our grandeur. Here are two completely different approaches: Shakespeare on the one hand, and Jeremiah on the other. While Jeremiah finds it impossible to stay convincingly with exploration of his feelings, the post-Renaissance poet finds it very difficult to speak convincingly of God. In *Paradise Lost*, Milton's picture of Satan is breathtaking, but his description of God falls flat—there is not the same wind in the sails as in Jeremiah's sails. This does not come from a lack of faith or of commitment—it simply comes from having started in the world in which Milton was set. That world determines where the power and energy are, and in the world of Shakespeare and Milton the real power is fascination with humanity. That is the driving force, not God. We ourselves are still in that world, and so we do not have it in us to live and speak as one of the Old Testament prophets, whose overriding interest is not humans but God—we are simply unconvincing when we try to do so.

Despite this unavoidable reality, many Christians sense a need today for Jeremiah's end of the picture. We are so human-centred that we have lost a vigorous sense of the sovereign call of God. The one is not better than the other, however. If we turn to the New Testament, we can, surprisingly, see both: we are not faced with a choice between these two poles. Jesus speaks with the voice of a prophet—without question, Jesus' words and actions proclaim the sovereign call of God, and they are convincing, more so than Milton's. Yet at the same time

---

[39] Farrer, *The Glass of Vision*, p. 125.

our ordinary humanity is basic for Jesus: people's lives, their struggles, sorrows, enjoyment of meals, enjoyment of jokes, sometimes killingly funny, their everyday occupations and loves. While the Old Testament prophets spoke to Israel and its vocation as a people, Jesus speaks to every person as a human being, but within a call to become a people of a new sort. He brings together the person, the community, and the divine. We can see the grasping of this very early on in St Augustine, whose wonderfully human autobiography, the *Confessions*, maps the journey Augustine makes from being centred on his humanity to being centred on God, in the divine/human community of the Church. Once the Church became accepted by the secular power, this higher unity that Jesus brought was split: it survived all the way through in individuals and groups, but there was a backtrack by the state, which lost sight of Jesus' radical compassion and non-violence, and this boomeranged to compromise the life and witness of the Church. Some have spoken of the period of Christendom from the Emperor Constantine until modern times as a time of "Mosaic Christianity", a Christianity that in many ways returned to Moses and the Old Testament, reading the words of Jesus in church but disregarding them in institutional violence, sitting in judgement on others, immorality and injustice. Only today are we beginning to see a serious return to what Jesus proclaims, in hopes for a more compassionate society.

We are in a difficult position—like Milton, we struggle to speak convincingly of God because our modern culture is in our grain. Perhaps we need a therapy, gradual formation in the micro-climate of the Church, the Holy Spirit inducting us into Jesus' way. For what we see in Jesus is not two poles, prophet and human being, but a unity, in singleness of heart.

1 0

Monastery and parish

We have made a journey through a variety of topics, all of them interlocking, and have repeatedly found, as we have gone along, ways in which the parish and religious communities share the same territory. In recent years, many have scratched their heads in trying to identify what is unique about the life of religious communities, because it is impossible to identify any single thing that is not done by other people too. There are Christians who are celibate, Christians who live obedient lives, or live simply, or stay in one place, or live in a community of some sort. And yet monastic life is distinctive enough for some people to talk about it as a sacrament. One thing you can say is that it brings together all the bits—it seeks to live all those things and not a selection. Secondly, as Rowan Williams suggests, monasticism is unique as a form of community that relies entirely upon the gospel for existing as a community: all other forms of human relating are cast into the shadow, such as family, career, commitment to self (see p.15). And yet this tough gospel call is for everybody, and all Christians are challenged to live it in a way that fits their circumstances. Thirdly, there is the fact that these people live within a unique framework, the monastic life and its tradition. We have spoken above of the "life" being bigger than the people who are living it, and that there are times when you feel monastic life does its stuff for the Church despite the people who are trying to live it. This way of life is a stylized activity, like a dance: once you step into the dance you sense it has a life of its own and is enlarging you. This "life" of religious communities, we need to be clear, is not something abstract—it is down to earth: a repertoire of practices, wisdom, insights, writings, places, stories, buildings, biographies, developed and refined over many centuries, tried, tested and sifted. This life, with its divine hinterland, is bigger than the people who are seeking to live it. And yet the same can be said of the parish and every Christian community. When we go to church we are not simply on a quest for things we cannot see—we are laying ourselves open to the effect on us of things and people we can see, hear, smell and touch, in an ensemble of things that is bigger than we are.

So we have these two things: the life of religious communities is unique, but it has something to share with all Christians at every point in their lives. Every community has its Rule, but that is always secondary, for our fundamental rule is always the gospel. All that religious communities are trying to do is to live the gospel.

One of the sacraments

Some recent writers have returned to the ancient understanding of monastic life as a sacrament. They say we need to go behind the medieval narrowing-down of the number of sacraments to seven, and the later Protestant slimming to two. St Augustine listed monastic life among a large number of sacraments; Pseudo-Dionysus (fifth century) included it in his list of six, Peter Damian (eleventh century) in his list of 14, and Hugh of St Victor (twelfth century) in his still longer list. In Eastern Orthodoxy, the monastic profession is understood as an ordination. An important contribution here has been a rediscovery of the early understanding of sacraments themselves as deriving from the notion of "mystery" found in the New Testament. In Orthodoxy still today, the sacraments are called "mysteries", while there is no word for "sacrament"—I have written extensively on this subject in my book *Pursuing the Mystery*.[40] Fundamentally Christ, the primordial Mystery of the New Testament, is hidden, as we have seen, in the world—he is there in the secular world and its daily life. It is in the Church that the wraps are taken off and Christ is fully revealed and named. In this way, the Church itself is seen as Sacrament or Mystery, and all of its life partakes of the sacramental dimension.

---

[40]   George Guiver, *Pursuing the Mystery: Worship and Daily Life as Presences of God* (London: SPCK, 1996; Mirfield Publications, 2016).

Being a model

Religious communities would hold their hands up in horror at any thought of holding themselves up as an example to anybody. A fundamental refrain for every member is, "I am a sinner and nothing without God." We should not caricature nuns or monks as goody-goodies—once our Superior was reading to us at Compline from a book by Michael Casey. At a certain point Casey said, "Every monastery has its crook," and all the brothers instantly looked at a particular brother.

This is one reason why seeing the life as a sacrament can be helpful. The monastic life itself is an example to absolutely everybody, both to normal Christians and to monastics themselves. It is only with this clearly in mind that we are able to speak of religious communities having things to share with the wider Church. So Karl Barth has written approvingly of monastic life as having over the centuries succeeded in "living faith and works in the right sequence"[41]—in other words, putting God before anything else (more specifically, God's Word—not just the written word, but the life of God coming to us through it). One way Barth believes religious communities are exemplary is the way they have repeatedly reformed and renewed themselves through history. He wrote in a letter to the Abbot of Montserrat in Spain that "their particular monastic existence stands and falls by the fact that their Lord, who is always faithful to himself and to this extent also to them, wills them, establishes them and orders them anew at every moment and in every situation."[42] St Benedict says this in his own way when he speaks of the monastery as a school in the Lord's service.[43] He applies it to the community members, but it can be applied to all. There is something in monastic life for all to sit under. Luigi Gioia, in commenting on Barth's views, says, "The exemplary role of monasticism [witnesses to] the infallible power of God's grace and mercy in the midst of an ever-increasing awareness of human opposition

---

[41] Karl Barth, *Church Dogmatics* IV.2 (Peabody, MA: Hendrickson, 2010), p. 18.

[42] Karl Barth, *Visioni attuali sulla vita monastica* (Barcelona: Abadía de Montserrat, 1966), pp. 43f.

[43] Rule of St Benedict, *Prologue* v. 45.

to it. It is precisely this tension, this paradox, that explains, for Barth, the fruitfulness of monasticism and its extraordinary resilience in spite of all its shortcomings."[44] For the Austrian abbot Bernard Eckerstorfer, religious communities are a symbol of the presence of God. He is using the word symbol here in its richer sense of something that touches the imagination, evoking realities that are beyond words. This chimes in with people's comments about the climate in religious communities, and with what we have been saying about the imagination—monastic life is like a work of art.

Difficult to see

If it is "the life" that is setting something before the rest of the Church, the brothers and sisters living that life can find it difficult to see all this. We go with a degree of not-seeing. St Augustine said that the mind is not large enough to contain itself[45]—I cannot totally grasp all that I am. Just as I cannot see the back of my head, so my mind is not big enough to see my full dimensions. Kierkegaard says of St Paul that the call to be an apostle is a paradoxical occurrence, lying always beyond his personal self-identity.[46] It is worth reading that sentence more than once. Being a nun or monk, or a Christian of any sort, is always paradoxical, lying beyond what we can see of ourselves. Thus we go always in faith when weighing up our own monastery, community or parish. What a religious community or a parish sees of itself can be discouraging, but there is more than we can see.

Here we encounter the visible and the invisible. You will not find anyone in a religious community who believes that what you see is everything. We have already heard how physical realities can channel the invisible. There are some religious communities that are "enclosed"—that

---

44 Luigi Gioia, *The Wisdom of St Benedict: Monastic Spirituality and the Life of the Church* (Norwich: Canterbury Press, 2020), pp. 137f.

45 Augustine, *Confessions*, 8.15.

46 Karl Barth, *The Epistle to the Romans* (Oxford: Oxford University Press, 1933), p. 27.

is, their members go outside the monastery very rarely, practising a strong form of being apart from the world. They force us to turn our attention towards the divine "economy"—the invisible working of God in the world. Religious communities by their prayer feed into the divine economy—what could be called God's hidden plumbing system going throughout the world. Unseen, all the prayer contributes to guiding the world on its path. The rabbis say that where one person is praying, a thousand people around them are saved. Religious community members believe prayer is effective, and contributes to life—to put it crudely, we could say God practises self-limitation, so that our prayer puts resources into God's hands. We can't see it, and there is precious little to prove it, but it is an inevitable corollary of giving yourself to life in a religious community—you simply know it as a living thing. This can help us see that all prayer by all people feeds into God's plumbing system. All prayer does something—we usually can't see it, but we come to know it. Furthermore, such prayer is not simply utilitarian—it is good because it is good, and loved because it is loved. We all sense it—"please pray for me", says someone with a medical problem; please pray for so-and-so who is in trouble, asks another. The requests pour in, and the intercession carries something that is believed, even by people who rarely go to church.

All other considerations apart, even if they seem to be achieving nothing else, religious communities are there because they pray. This prayer is like a pilot light in a gas appliance, keeping the flame burning, however much the rest may flicker or go out. People often have a sense of religious communities being places where the faith becomes more believable, where orthodox Christian faith comes alive again for those undermined by contemporary culture, where the faith-imagination is touched. It is sometimes said that even though a person may never have visited a religious community, the fact that they exist, that some people are able to give their lives to Christian faith in this way, helps to make Christianity more believable. If monks and nuns can do all this and not go mad or look patent frauds, there must be something in it. Linked to this is the sense that in any diocese, in any area, the religious communities (if there are such) are a city of refuge, a hearth always burning—somebody is there 24/7, and in times of emergency or unexpected need they can be turned to. Nuns and monks, however, never lay claim to any of this—all we can do is try to serve it. Yet again you have to go on and say that every parish is summoned to be such a place, where prayer is believable, and the faith imagination is touched, a secure place that is simply there.

Imitation

If it is possible to talk about monastic life as an exemplar, we need to be careful not to see it as a model to imitate. Some forms of imitation can help us on the Christian way—after all, we are told, "Christ also suffered for you, leaving you an example, so that you should follow in his steps" (1 Peter 2:21). An old piece of advice, if we cannot love someone, is to "do what love would do", and love will grow. We have to keep an eye out for pitfalls, however, despite the popularity of Thomas a Kempis' *The Imitation of Christ*. This is because imitation implies a copying of what we see, using our own individual abilities. Imitation is profitable when it is about seeking to learn, seeking a leg-up, but less helpful when aimed simply at reproducing what we think we see. The gospel has little to say about imitation, but a lot to say about life in Christ, and Christ at work in us. If there is to be talk of the life of religious communities providing an example for the Church, we can be helped to understand that by asking what visitors say. Often people say the most important thing about it is very simple: a community of brothers, sisters, in their church/chapel praying; they may also speak of the particular ministry of that community. If communities are holding something before the Church, it may be something we sense, that is beyond words, beyond our ability simply to imitate. A perfume, as some of the saints might have said, rather than a list of things to try and reproduce.

The Church, its people and liturgy and practices, have a givenness like the sea—the power and constant energy of the sea's swell is an apt image of this loving and serving life which, like that ever-flowing sea, is simply, vibrantly there.

If we persevere trustingly in it, we shall suddenly come to see. You perform it all, you live the living Tradition, in the Holy Spirit, and, behind this performing, Christ communicates with and transforms you. As

Richard Rohr has said of life in the Catholic tradition, "Once you get it, there is no going back, because nothing is better than this."[47]

> Lord, your silence seems empty . . .
> Where are you?
> How can I launch out from the confines of my head?
> You send back to me a different question –
> "Can I come in?"
> But how can I let you in? How do I hear and see you?
> Can the senses find you?
> Can my touch, sight, hearing be awoken by you?
> Now . . .
> People have been around me all the time
> and I haven't sensed you in them.
> Church buildings, font and altar,
> Scripture, poetry, prayers,
> music, beauty,
> icons,
> liturgy, sacraments,
> community,
> love,
> mirrorings of sacrifice and resurrection
> in loving lives,
> the Church's mystery,
> the gathering-up of the Eucharist,
> profundity of inheritance handed on,
> the audacious shock of Christ's incarnation
> bridging the impossible gap.
> I cannot claim I touch and see,
> and yet I know in these
> my touch is met,
> I hear, see and sense
> I am set somewhere not nowhere
> —"it is good to be here"—

---

47   Richard Rohr, *Falling Upwards* (San Francisco: Jossey-Bass, 2011), p. 76.

not I but we,

community in communion,

sings, feels, smells and swims with fleshly being,

a dance,

Father, Son and Holy Spirit.

Your silence

is no empty gift,

but full,

setting me, setting us—here.

For further reading

Matthew Crawford, *The World Beyond Your Head* (London: Penguin, 2016).

Charles Cummings, *Monastic Practices*, revised edition (Collegeville, MN: Liturgical Press, 2015).

George Guiver, *Company of Voices: Daily Prayer and the People of God*, revised edition (Norwich: Canterbury Press, 2001).

George Guiver, *Everyday God*, 3rd edition (Mirfield: Mirfield Publications, 2015).

Fraser Watts, *A Plea for Embodied Spirituality* (London: SCM Press, 2021).

"Can these stones come alive?"

In Chapter 8, there was brief mention of developments in the parish of the Sacred Heart in Trier, Germany. There was not space there to say more, although those developments are of considerable interest to our topic. Here the parish priest, Ralf Schmitz, has written a report on the parish's journey over the last few years. You might be interested to see how many themes from this book you can identify in it (see <https//sredna-herzjesu.de>).

For almost 15 years, I had been living as pastor of the deaf community in the presbytery of the formerly independent parish of the Sacred Heart of Jesus in Trier, Germany. In 2003, it was integrated into the parish of St Matthias' Monastery, together with another. Parish life had largely come to a standstill. The reasons were complex. The social structure in the district had changed fundamentally. Many students had moved to the area. The number of people who had lived here for a long time was decreasing. An above-average number of artists who worked at the nearby theatre lived here. The "unchurching" may have progressed faster than in other parts of the city. Many residents worked in neighbouring Luxembourg and used the cheaper accommodation here without really integrating into local life. From a lively suburb community life in the 1970s and 1980s, all that was left was an ageing Catholic women's community. The only service was the Saturday evening vigil mass, which because of its early start at 5 p.m. also had an appeal beyond the area. For a long time, I assumed that the Sacred Heart Church would be the first in that part of Trier to be closed—the costs are out of all proportion to the benefits. Eight other parish and monastery churches are within a kilometre radius. The Cathedral can be reached on foot in just 20 minutes. The explosive nature of the question became clear: "Can the stones of the Sacred Heart of Jesus come to life?"

As in Ezekiel 37:3, I had the feeling that the question was directed at me: "Son of man, can these dry bones live again?" And my honest answer was: "You know that, only you, Lord!"

Signs of hope

At the very least, the answer could not be an unequivocal "no". There were also signs of hope. The church interior is bright and simple. It is particularly suitable for sign language services. As pastor of the deaf community, that was particularly important to me. Since 2003, we have been using the former presbytery of the Sacred Heart parish as our community centre—with an office and smaller meeting rooms, the pastor's apartment, a guest floor and a large garden. It took a while for the deaf community to get used to the new place. The advantages were obvious, at least for me: on a sunny Sunday, we don't need artificial lighting in the church. Visually the space is quite sparse, dominated by the red and blue chancel windows. Every small visual change caused by light, textiles, objects and pictures unfolds a different spatial effect and atmosphere. Over time, however, the deaf community became more than at home. The worship community was even more important than a friendly, inviting church interior. I sensed a great deal of openness and curiosity among many of the church service participants. They were survivors of the "congregational church" that had developed during the Second Vatican Council. The last pastor had shaped the congregation strongly in this direction—and the congregation followed the path with great conviction.

From the beginning, the deaf congregation and a residential community with people with intellectual disabilities from a neighbouring parish were very welcome in the integrative (later inclusive) services. The Easter Triduum was formative. In the first years after the parish merger, the services from Maundy Thursday to Easter were only held in the main church of St Matthias. The deaf community began celebrating its own service in sign language in 2005, with many elements of youth work. The core of the church service was a group of young deaf people who spent the entire Easter weekend together in our vicarage. Over the years, the number of non-deaf church participants has increased, so that today these services are fully inclusive: they are celebrated simultaneously and equally in signed and spoken language.

In 2017, two women from our congrergation visited the Augustinian Church in Würzburg. It had been reordered and was almost unrecognizable: the arrangement of the chairs and some other changes gave the space a whole new look. We thought: "We should try that here!" That was how the project was born: we wanted to find out what would happen if we rearranged the pews—and placed the altar and lectern in the middle of the church. The pews were easy to rearrange and set up between the four pillars in the nave. A blacksmith from the parish created four simple candlesticks that take up the shape of six large candlesticks in the choir. These four smaller candlesticks are easy to convert. With a frame and a glass plate, they form the altar in the nave. Simple in its form, provisional, transparent, and yet striking, it creates the focal point in the nave together with a similarly designed lectern and two candlesticks. The benches form a hexagon around this centre. "Give us 70 days, from Easter to the Feast of the Sacred Heart of Jesus!" I asked the worshipping community on Palm Sunday 2017. "After that we will put everything back and evaluate with you whether anything has changed and how we want to continue." We got that leap of faith—there were no complaints to the bishop. The marginal location of Herz Jesu in the parish of St Matthias and its marginal art-historical insignificance were a blessing. There were no discussions in the Parish Council, and we were able to experiment undisturbed in a church that shouldn't have even existed anymore.

"sredna—see, hear, taste differently"

The first project period began at Easter 2017. The "sredna" brand comes from the German word "anders" (=differently) written backwards. Inspired by the deaf community in particular, we wanted to enable spiritual experiences "with all senses". In the deaf community, it is unimaginable to celebrate a Sunday service without the "eighth sacrament" (coffee and cake) afterwards. People have often come a long way and enjoy the personal encounter. Another experience with the deaf community made an impression on me: one day a community festival was totally rained out and the vicarage garden could not be used for the festival after the service. A larger space was not within reach. So we moved to the church without further ado—under the gallery and in the side aisles. We turned a few pews, set up tables, and celebrated the "eighth sacrament" in the church. The participants were enthusiastic: "We will always have our garden party here in the future!" In the church, eyes and ears are addressed above all. "Tasting" is either reduced to the Eucharistic gifts or banned to outside the church door. It should be different with us. During the renovation of 1992/93, herbal and medicinal plant motifs were applied in the church by the parish artist Heinrich Feld: on the wooden ceiling in the vault, on the triumphal arch above the altar, on the front of the organ gallery, but above all on the Stations of the Cross. Medieval traditions and interpretations were incorporated; plants and herbs became symbols of the healing effects of Christ and his sacraments. One of the first events was entitled: "Olive tree—thistle—dandelion". Heinrich Feld took three Stations of the Cross and explained the plants and their meaning. The Regional Cantor Joachim Reidenbach improvised on the organ. Afterwards, dishes made from the plants mentioned were offered for tasting under the organ gallery. A first, very original experience under the heading "see, hear, taste differently".

Various other spiritual events with a cultural and a culinary dimension have been added over the years. The get-together "under the gallery" after the evening mass was fully established until the start of the Covid pandemic. With a glass of wine or soda, part of the congregation stays together for a while—preparation and follow-up are self-organized. The earlier Sacred Heart Festival, with a festive service and procession followed by a parish festival, had fallen asleep over the years due to a lack of participation and helpers. It was reborn, also as a parish festival, for the deaf community. The inclusive service in sign and spoken language was followed by a lively and light celebration in and around the church. When we wanted to put the pews back in the traditional order, there were protests from the traditional church community: "The pews should stay where they are now. We no longer want to give up the feeling of community in the service!" For two years, we lived with a compromise: outside the project period, the pews in the front part of the church were traditionally aligned, while in the back they stood in a U-shape. After a vote at the 2019 community festival, the community decided that the order of the benches would remain in the shape of the hexagon.

I would like to mention two experiences in particular: firstly, the 2019 Christmas mass, which was a very special experience. Then many "Sacred-Hearters" return to their families of origin, and it's important for them to see the old familiar places. But it was amazing how positively the new seating arrangement was received. The second experience was the first mass after the first Covid lockdown in 2020: despite the mandatory masks, the church service participants were able to look each other "in the eye". The feeling of community despite the distance was very comforting and continues to this day.

Spiritual—Creative—Inclusive—Neighbourly

After the first positive experiences and a new vitality in the church, further focal points developed. With his pastoral project on the spirituality of creation and some planted raised beds in front of the church, parish officer Heiko Paluch laid the foundation stone for the "Sacred Heart Garden" next to the church. Over the past three years a team has since turned an unused green strip alongside the church into a neighbourhood garden in the city. People from the neighbourhood who are only loosely connected to the worship community get involved here. Cooperation with local organizations and individuals meanwhile shapes life in the church and around it: events and projects with a secondary school, as well as a cult cocktail bar across the road, a neighbourhood bakery, the local AIDS charity, an LGBT+ centre, cultural workers from different contexts, the local advisory board all shape and influence the local network. The cooperation happens on an equal footing. We experience openness and curiosity. The aim is to help shape a fair, social, lively, and liveable district. The time when the Catholic Church dominated the district is long gone. Of course, there are also reservations about the church in the district. We benefit from the distinction between the church as an institution, as an organization and as a movement. As a "movement", we are thoroughly accepted. In the ecumenical spectrum, personal contacts have resulted in relationships with the New Apostolic Church and the Old Catholic Church. The catechumenate circle of the Deanery often takes part in church services—and brings its cultural diversity with it. Newly baptized Iranians helped organize many church services before they had to change their place of residence due to their asylum procedure. Since the beginning of 2020, "sredna Sacred Heart" has been a registered association in order to be economically independent and to give people the opportunity to participate who have difficulties with the officially constituted Catholic Church or who have left it. In the context of sredna, the "Cultural Diaconate Initiative in Trier South" was created in September 2020, a project funded by the Diocese of Trier that uses theatre and performing arts as a medium of spirituality and diaconal action personally and politically. Despite the Covid restrictions, a large number of "physical" and virtual events and projects have emerged. The interaction of art, culture and spirituality is experienced as enriching and inspiring by all those involved.

New liturgical experiences in the surrounding social context—in Covid times

A good four years ago, I asked the question: "Can these stones (from the heart of Jesus) come to life?" As of today I can say: yes, they are alive. And it's good that they exist. The neo-Gothic church building with its mighty, elegant tower and the lively garden around it at a prominent street crossing has its own dignity. It is an identification point in the district. The church is jokingly called "St Sredna".

Covid and its protective measures have brought us closer together with the Nelson-Mandela School, with the "South Pole" youth centre, with artists, with the AIDS charity, with various networks that meet in the church for meetings and events.

Our worship life has changed. In the summer of 2020, a team put together an exhibition about the former Sacred Heart Hospital, which brought many people to the church who had had anything to do with the hospital. The hospital was right next to the church. "Half of Trier" was born there. On the Saturdays, there was "table music" with organ music—prayer—soup with bread—organ music at the end. The other accompanying events also had a spiritual impulse again and again. Despite the Covid rules, the "tasting" should not be completely absent and often found very creative forms of expression.

"20-minutes-in-the-church" in Advent with the Nelson-Mandela School unexpectedly became a low-threshold place of support after a man ran amok with a lorry through crowds of pedestrians in Trier, killing six. Traumatized pupils with different cultural and religious backgrounds felt comforted and supported. A second series on the theme of "dignity" took place with the Misereor Lenten cloth (you can Google to learn about this). In a performance, groups of students brought the cloth from their schoolyard to the church and reflected on the injustice they had experienced themselves.

The Sunday services in Advent and at Christmas time became solidarity services with artists who were thrown into existential and economic difficulties by the pandemic. It was important to us that there should be an intensive interaction between dance, drama, unusual music on the one hand and liturgy on the other hand—to texts from the prophet Isaiah.

The "Happening & Soup" series on Saturday afternoon has been accompanying the "Dignity!!! I—You—We" performance with 15 participants by Ralf Knoblauch. What does indignity mean at the end of life, for women in distress, for children, for sex workers, for refugees— and how can dignity be restored? The content of the contributions is embedded in music and prayer, and at the end there is soup to take away since, with Covid, eating together in the church was not possible.

The "Pray-phone" has been around for three years now—daily at eight in the morning and at seven in the evening. Between five and ten people pray together over the medium of the telephone. Lyrics and songs can be found on our website. For many months, we have celebrated a Sunday service as a "vigil service" (during the first lockdown) and then as a "morning service" on Sunday morning as a video or telephone conference. People from all over Germany join in. The themes and texts from the "physical" services in the Sacred Heart Church are often taken up.

The "Queer Night Prayer" takes place about four times a year. It is designed by a preparatory team with elements of LGBT+ spirituality and is primarily aimed at queer people, couples and families. Of course, the service is inclusive—everyone is welcome. Occasionally it is also translated into sign language. During the lockdown times, the prayer took place online twice. Trier AIDS-Help has held a solidarity night several times in front of and in the church. Here, too, the encounter "under the gallery" is an integral part of the service.

In the meantime, the Trier Sant'Egidio community prays regularly in our church and often takes part in festive services.

Fragments of the living in new liturgical experiences

The new liturgical life is selective, fleeting, personal and project-related. The shared adventures and experiences change perspectives and opinions, in the best case on all sides. It takes a lot of energy and willingness to communicate. It takes a basic attitude of openness and modesty to get involved in the social space and its processes—as one player among many. We have to treat those with respect and, if necessary, let them have their say who simply don't want to have anything to do with religion, belief and especially with the church. It requires willingness to experiment and to take risks; an acceptance of imperfection; the willingness to set off without knowing where the journey is going. It takes an understanding of tradition that is not about guarding the ashes, but passing on the flame.

A new liturgy emerges when a worshipping community engages with the local social space in which it lives and for which it is there. Liturgy grows out of *diakonia*—and not only through intercessions and the collection. A new liturgy is emerging in new forms of communion—physically, online or on the phone. Conversely, new communities are also expressed in new liturgies. The church building itself was open daily from morning to evening through the pandemic—and has become a place for individual forms of prayer and worship.

The theologian Fulbert Steffensky was a guest for a "table talk" in September 2020. His theme was "Fragments of Hope". Culture and thus spirituality are not planned processes. They are fragments. They consist of detours, duplications, overlapping elements, and interpretations that do not follow a straight line, but simply come together, complement each other, stand side by side without relation, or even contradict each other. But in this way they open up a space of ambiguity that enables diversity, tolerance, encounters and creative development.

"Can these stones come to life?"—That was the initial question of the church project "sredna—see, hear, taste differently" at Easter 2017. What subsequently developed was not the result of a structured planning process. We found ourselves more in the three-step "start—evaluate—change" (Dave Snowden's Cynefin model). The developments were often not planned and not foreseeable. The management team was curious about what was offered. We are eager to see what happens. "I will open your graves and bring you up, my people, from your graves (. . .). I will breathe my spirit into you, then you will come alive (. . .). I have spoken and I will do it—says the Lord" (Ezekiel 37:12–14).

Ralf Schmitz